The Great Northern M_

Ken and Jean Smith

This book is dedicated to the memory of all miners who lost their lives in the pits of the North East
or who died from an illness or injury resulting from their work in those pits.

Tyne Bridge Publishing

Acknowledgements

Newcastle Libraries extend warm thanks to Thompsons Solicitors and to Elanders Hindson for their generous support of the production of this book.

We must also thank Ian Lavery of the NUM; Sue Coulthard, NCC; Jennifer Kelly, Librarian, North of England Institute of Mining and Mechanical Engineers; Liz Rees, Tyne & Wear Archives Service; Anthea Lang, Gateshead Libraries & Arts; the Ashington Group Trustees; Beamish Open Air Museum; Hatton Gallery, Newcastle University; Live Theatre; Literary and Philosophical Society of Newcastle upon Tyne; Northern Echo; Northumberland Record Office; ncjMedia; Yorkshire Post; and all the many other researchers and contributors who have generously given their time and support (authors' acknowledgements on page 189).

Illustrations

New photography is by Tom Yellowley and Richard Smith.

Archive illustrations are reproduced from the collections of Newcastle Libraries, unless otherwise indicated.

Published by
City of Newcastle upon Tyne
Newcastle Libraries & Information Service
Tyne Bridge Publishing

www.tynebridgepublishing.co.uk

ISBN 978 185795 119 6

Printed by Elanders Hindson, North Tyneside

Ken Smith is a sub-editor on *The Journal*, Newcastle, and his wife, Jean, is a retired Newcastle Community midwife.

For other titles by Ken Smith see www.tynebridgepublishing.co.uk

Front cover: Miners leaving Charlotte Pit, Benwell, 1929. (*West Newcastle Local Studies*)

Back cover: a pitwheel at Ashington QEII Country Park. (*Tom Yellowley*)

Definitions at the beginning of some chapters are taken from *Glossary of terms used in the Coal Trade* by G.C. Greenwell, 1888.

A miner, in his pit clothes, carrying his tools, from 'The Miners' Advocate' 1843-1845. It depicts: 'the collier in one of the most laborious of his occupations – viz.: removing his tools.'

The views expressed in this book are those of the authors and contributors, and in no way reflect the views of Tyne Bridge Publishing or the Council of the City of Newcastle upon Tyne.

Contents

Wanted, AT WASHINGTON COLLIERY, 100 Hewers, AND A PROPORTIONABLE NUMBER OF PUTTERS, And other Boys. Such Men as are at perfect Liberty to fulfil the Engagements they may enter into with the Owners, will meet with every Encouragement and Protection. Application to be made to Mr. Morris, at the Colliery Office. N. B. Good and comfortable Houses adjoining each other, are now ready for Workmen. Washington Colliery, July 13th, 1832. JOHN LOWTHIN, PRINTER, GATESHEAD.

North of England Institute of Mining and Mechanical Engineers WAT-1-28-21

'Tyne river, running rough or smooth,
Brings bread to me and mine;
Of all the rivers north or south
There's none like coaly Tyne.'

(Traditional Tyneside song)

ncjMedia / The Journal

*Smiling miners leave
Ravensworth Colliery, near
Birtley, after a Saturday
morning shift in 1951.*

The Great Northern Miners – an introduction by Ian Lavery

I am always pleased to be asked to contribute to any historical portrait of the coal industry and especially to remember those great men the miners themselves who worked in the most hazardous of conditions to secure a better future for us all.

The Great Northern Miners describes a most varied way of life of miners and their families within the great Northern Region of Northumberland and Durham, highlighting the political and industrial struggle endured right from the time of Henry III in 1239 to the present day.

The book illustrates how the collective action of suppressed workers, and in most cases entire communities, can develop and thrive with a true sense of purpose and social spirit. It is endearing to read the words of the elderly miners as they express in detail their extreme pride in their mining heritage and in the very fact that they were miners. They remember the dark days, the tragedies, the death and mayhem but also their friends and comrades, the good times, the laughs, the crack, and not least the camaraderie which was synonymous with coal mining.

Chapter Three refers to the 'bond system' – quite simply another name for slavery. Miners were tied to one employer, often working in conditions unfit for any normal human being and often unpaid for the privilege. Miners faced eviction and prison sentences if they attempted to break their bond. The bond itself created immense problems resulting in many violent disputes between the unions and the employers; thankfully it was abolished in 1872. I merely highlight this as one of the cruellest acts one individual can force onto another. It brings tears to my eyes to think what those decent individuals had to endure in order to provide food and drink for their families. The 'bond system' was a despicable episode in the history of our industry.

The Great Northern Miners is published at a time when the world is facing a global energy crisis.

For the first time in history the UK as a nation is a net importer of our energy needs. Coal is used to produce on average 35% of our electricity requirements, yet we choose to destroy our coal industry and import 50 million tonnes of coal on an annual basis. World coal production is set to dramatically increase between now and 2030 mainly due to the rapid industrialisation of the tiger economy India and China.

Coal can be burned cleanly with near zero emissions. We have millions of tonnes beneath our feet and we have an experienced workforce with the skills and technology to mine coal both safely and competitively. I think we should learn from the experiences relayed in this book to expand our coal industry once again, be self sufficient and build on the struggles of the past.

Coal is not the dirty fuel of the past – coal is the clean fuel of the future.

Ian Lavery, February 2008
President of the National Union of Mineworkers
General Secretary of the Northumberland Miners

Symbol of a rich mining heritage. A pitwheel overlooks the Queen Elizabeth II Country Park, Ashington, opened in 1979. The park area was once part of a vast colliery spoil tip.

Won from the Earth

'Pit: A circular, oval, square, or oblong, vertical sinking from the surface.'

Today there are few traces left in North East England of coal mining, that once great industry which was the region's lifeblood. Coal dominated the economy of the area and many of its communities depended on it for their livelihoods. The dusty 'black diamonds' exported for centuries from the North East coast were truly the foundation stone of the region's industrial development and of its population growth.

There are very few surviving pithead winding wheels still in their original position. However, two towers with their pairs of wheels stand at the site of Woodhorn Colliery, now the Woodhorn Museum and Archives Centre, on the outskirts of Ashington, Northumberland. They are rare reminders of an era when vast numbers of men toiled underground to win the coal from the black depths beneath the streets and fields.

Another pair of wheels with their Victorian winding engine survive at the site of the Washington F Pit on Wearside. At South Shields, a pair can be seen atop the rear of a mine building housing a shaft at the location of the St Hilda Colliery. A considerable number of other wheels have been erected as memorials. But that is all. Yet once these pulley wheels and their engine houses dotted the region's landscape in profusion.

Nor today are there many slag or spoil heaps visible – those numerous hills of coaly waste which were so prominent on the northern skyline, smoky as the result of internal combustion and sometimes glowing at night. A number have been landscaped, being turned into green hills, and many others have been removed or smoothed away as the result of reclamation schemes.

Except for a few working opencast sites, most signs of mining have been erased from the North East scene and the world of the miner, once the most familiar of North East figures, has vanished. To past generations it would have seemed unimaginable that the region could be bereft of its pits and pitmen. Yet far beneath the fields and streets the mine workings extend for countless miles, unseen as we go about our daily lives. Many are filled with water.

Although the Romans are known to have extracted coal in the North East, the history of mining in the region as a continuous, organised industry stretches back for around 800 years to Medieval times. There is at least one record of mining from the late 12th century in County Durham. Coal is known to have been mined in the Tyneside area as early as the first half of the 13th century (the 1200s). From this century onwards the black diamonds were exported from the Tyne in small sailing ships which came to be known as 'colliers'. Much of the coal was carried south through the coastal waters of the North Sea to London. There it was known as 'sea coal' – it came to the capital by sea. However, the term may originally have been applied to coal collected after it was washed up on North East beaches from the undersea measures or where it outcropped on the shore.

Initially, coal was easily found on or near the surface and the first North East pits – bell-pits – were therefore extremely shallow by later standards. These earliest mines were simple enough affairs. A shaft was excavated to a depth of less than 100ft and the coal was dug from the sides of the pit bottom. When it was unsafe to undermine the rock further because the overhanging roof was in danger of collapse, the pit, which had assumed a roughly bell-like shape, was abandoned and work began on excavating another. Alternatively, if the coal outcropped on a hill or slope a short tunnel – known as a drift – could be started by digging horizontally or at a slight incline into the seam.

The sites of bell pits are sometimes detectable today. The remains of two bell pits dating back to the first half of the 17th century were discovered in a field at Lottie's Wood, East Sunniside Farm, Sunniside, Gateshead. An information plaque was unveiled at the site in 2007.

In October 2007 a section of the Tyne and Wear Metro train line was temporarily closed when subsidence occurred at the trackside between Northumberland Park and Shiremoor stations in North Tyneside. It was reported that a hole had developed due to old bell pit workings. Repairs followed.

The black diamonds were mined both north and south of the Tyne. Coal even outcropped on Newcastle's Town Moor and was also found at The Forth, a green area outside the town walls. In 1239 Henry III granted permission to the Newcastle townsmen to dig for coal and over a century later, in 1351, Edward III granted a similar permission for mining on the Town Moor and The Forth. The monks of Tynemouth are also believed to have mined coal and may

The top of a shaft, a horse-gin for raising the coals, corves and waggonway horses with full chaldron waggons can be seen in this print from c1800.

have shipped it from Prior's Haven, a small bay at the mouth of the river, from the 1260s onwards.

The importance of the industry continued to grow. By the mid-16th century a booming trade in coals had developed. This was a century of expansion for coal mining in the region. For example, in the year ending Michaelmas 1592 in the reign of Elizabeth I, a total of 91,420 tons of black diamonds was shipped on coastal routes from the Tyne, much of it going to the growing London market where coal was increasingly burned instead of wood to warm homes. In earlier times wood had been the preferred fuel for home fires, with coal being used for industrial purposes such as lime burning and brewing, but by the Elizabethan period a shortage of timber brought about a gradual switch to coal.

The Dissolution of the Monasteries in 1536-1539 had given an enormous impetus to the industry in the Tyneside area, since mining output on church-owned lands had hitherto been restricted by the monasteries to conserve stocks. The church was a major landowner. Following the Dissolution, those lands were confiscated by the Crown and leased out to entrepreneurs without any limit on output. The trade was boosted and in 1600 Elizabeth I granted the Hostmen of Newcastle, the town coal merchants' guild, a charter to take sole control of shipments of black diamonds from the Tyne.

The amount of coal leaving the river continued to increase in the 17th century. For example, in 1633-34 the total reached 452,625 tons. Much of the coal at this stage came from pits north and south of the Tyne in the area immediately to the west of Newcastle, but in the 18th century a considerable number of collieries also opened nearer the river mouth, to the east.

Shallow bell-pits proved to be a passing phase. As the higher deposits of coal were worked out shafts were sunk to deeper seams and with increasing depth two major dangers were encountered – gas and water.

Methane gas, or firedamp as it is known to miners, led to numerous explosions in which large numbers of men and boys died. Added to this, carbon monoxide gas, known as afterdamp, could develop as an after-effect of an explosion and this caused further loss of life. Other problems included chokedamp (also known as

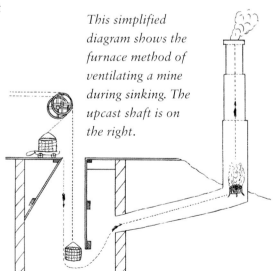

This simplified diagram shows the furnace method of ventilating a mine during sinking. The upcast shaft is on the right.

blackdamp) when there was a high level of carbon dioxide and a low level of oxygen in the air (sometimes present after explosions), hydrogen sulphide gas, known as stinkdamp, and stythe gas which occurs near the floor of workings.

Firedamp explosions frequently resulted from miners using candles or unprotected oil flames. Such naked lights were a great peril and Tyneside was noted for its gaseous seams. The deaths of men and boys as the result of blasts caused by this fatal combination of naked lights and gas led to the invention of the Geordie and Davy safety lamps in the early 19th century. These lamps were designed to protect the flame from the explosive effects of methane. But they gave a poor light and miners still frequently used candles or unprotected oil flames because they were paid according to the amount of coal they could win from the seams.

An initial firedamp blast might set off a further explosive episode triggered by coal dust. In such a case the explosion of dust could sweep through a mine in a wave of fiery detonation which often caused great loss of life. Shot-firing operations could act upon the coal dust to similar destructive effect, for coal dust on its own could be explosive, although this was not fully understood in early years.

It was soon realised as the pits grew deeper in the 18th century that an efficient system of ventilation was necessary to keep the air flowing through a mine so that 'foul' air such as methane and carbon dioxide was expelled and did not have time to build up.

An early method of ventilation involved equipping a mine with two shafts – the upcast and the downcast. A fire was lit in a furnace at the bottom of the upcast shaft or suspended in an iron brazier in the shaft. The fire would draw air up the shaft, thus expelling dangerous gases and at the same time sucking fresh air down the downcast shaft and into the mine. Air was thus kept flowing through the workings. Sometimes a mine had only one shaft and the upcast and downcast airways were contained within the same shaft, being divided by wooden partitioning (bratticing).

However, a system of 'trap' doors between intake and outflow airways within the mine was needed to make the upcast and downcast system work safely, thus avoiding the danger of gases building up in parts of the workings. Eventually, systems were devised whereby the fresh air drawn into a mine via the downcast shaft was split between the working areas.

The 19th century witnessed the gradual replacement of the furnace method. From the 1860s onwards large mechanical fans were introduced into pits for ventilation. These expelled the air via chimneys, still using the upcast and downcast shafts system.

Flooding was also a lethal peril for miners. Underground water was sometimes encountered at great pressure and might burst through on to unsuspecting men from old, abandoned workings which had become flooded. This was not the only such problem – workings could simply be 'drowned out' from water accumulated in layers of rock or sand seeping downwards, causing extensive flooding and resulting in closure of the pit.

Against this background, systems for pumping out mines were essential. The use of horse-power to draw up buckets of water and later to work pumps was employed extensively in early pits, but this was far from satisfactory. Some mines also used waterwheels for pumping if practicable. However, a

A type of horse-gin or whim-gin used for winding operations.

great step forward came in 1712 when Thomas Newcomen's atmospheric pressure pumping engine, which worked by means of a moving beam, was first used at a colliery. This engine was a much more effective way of keeping the water level down. Newcomen's invention enabled deeper seams to be worked in the North East. In the second half of the 19th century other, more efficient pumping engines, worked by steam, came into use.

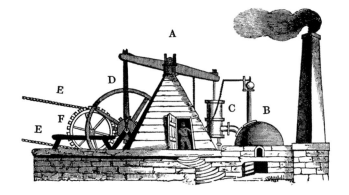

A steam engine used for raising corves or pumping water, known as a 'whim' or 'whimsey' from John Holland's Fossil Fuel, 1841.

Horse-gins (also called whim-gins) were generally used for shaft winding operations, both for men and coal, during the 17th and 18th centuries. This involved attaching a horse to a horizontal winding drum.

A major advance occurred in 1800 when Phineas Crowther, of Heaton, Newcastle, patented a vertical single-cylinder steam winding engine and this came to be adopted by most pits in the North East. The vertical layout of this machinery with the winding wheel placed above the cylinder led to the tall appearance of many engine houses throughout the region. In the 20th century steam driven machinery was gradually replaced by electrically operated winding. However, steam winding lasted at a few pits until the 1960s and at Woodhorn Colliery in Northumberland until 1975.

Mines also needed efficient systems of transport. Horse-drawn carts (wains) and packhorses were the earliest means of carrying the coal on the surface. But the 17th century witnessed a gradual change in methods. In c1605-08 the earliest horse-drawn wooden waggonways to transport coal in the North East were opened near the River Blyth. Waggonways were to supersede the wain and packhorse which were impeded by the appalling state of roads and tracks.

By the second half of the 18th century a large number of these waggonways laid with wooden rails had been created to take the coal from the pits to staiths on the rivers Tyne and Wear. Staiths were wooden riverside jetties or

An illustration from John Brand's History of Newcastle (1789) shows Newcastle's 18th century stone bridge of arches. A waggon of coal, with a horse driver sitting on the brake shaft, eases gently down the gradient towards the Tyne. The horse follows behind.

platforms from which the dusty cargo was loaded for onward shipment. They were also found on the River Blyth and were installed at other harbours of the North East, including, in the 19th century, Seaham and West Hartlepool.

The development of early waggonways was a portent of the steam-powered revolution to come. Bridges and cuttings were sometimes built for the waggonways where denes, rivers and hills intervened. The most famous example of this is the impressive single-span Causey Arch, the world's oldest surviving railway bridge, built in the 1720s near Stanley, County Durham, to carry a waggonway across the dene of the Causey Burn.

The horse-drawn waggons used on the wooden rails came to have a distinctive shape, being wider at the top than the bottom so that the black diamonds would drop down easily. The waggons were known as 'chaldrons' after the measure of coal they contained.

Causey Arch, near Stanley, the world's oldest surviving railway bridge. It was built in 1725-6.

Iron rails first appeared on a North East waggonway in the 1790s and by the early 19th century were catching on fast. By the 1840s virtually all the North East's railways, as the waggonways were by then known, had converted to this more durable and efficient material. Wooden rails were consigned to history.

Alongside this development, men such as William Chapman, John Blenkinsop, Matthew Murray, William Hedley, Timothy Hackworth and best known of all, George Stephenson, had from c1812-16 made the North East coal waggonways the main testing ground for a new form of transport, the steam locomotive. The iron rail made this possible.

The travelling engine, the name sometimes given to the steam locomotive, was pioneered against the background of the Napoleonic Wars when horses were scarce and fodder very expensive. The development of the locomotive was driven by the need to transport coal as cheaply as possible to the staiths of the North East, making the region the 'cradle of the railways'. Although the steam locomotive was invented by Cornishman Richard Trevithick, it was in the North East that men such as George Stephenson took up Trevithick's initial spark of ingenuity and honed it into workable form.

The evolution of the waggonway system from horse to steam power, from wooden to iron rails, went hand in hand with the growing output of the region's pits. This coal poured forth in a vast, seemingly endless stream which fuelled the Industrial Revolution.

By 1900 a vast railway network covered the North East, with lines from virtually every colliery connected to the staiths on the rivers or at the harbours. It was here that ships, bound for destinations worldwide, loaded the dark gems won by the hard labour of the pitmen. The black diamonds from the Great Northern Coalfield were dull and without sparkle but were nevertheless a precious stone, providing civilisation with an asset of incalculable worth.

The North East was one of the first coalfields to be developed on a large scale. Its assets were abundant. The output of Northumberland and Durham was also versatile – coals for raising steam to drive industrial machinery, to drive locomotives and ships, for household fires, for coking, for gas and, in later years, for electricity generation were all found in the region. This land between the Tweed and Tees was in the premier league for supplying the world, yet its miners faced a daily battle with danger to wrest that coveted mineral from the deep earth.

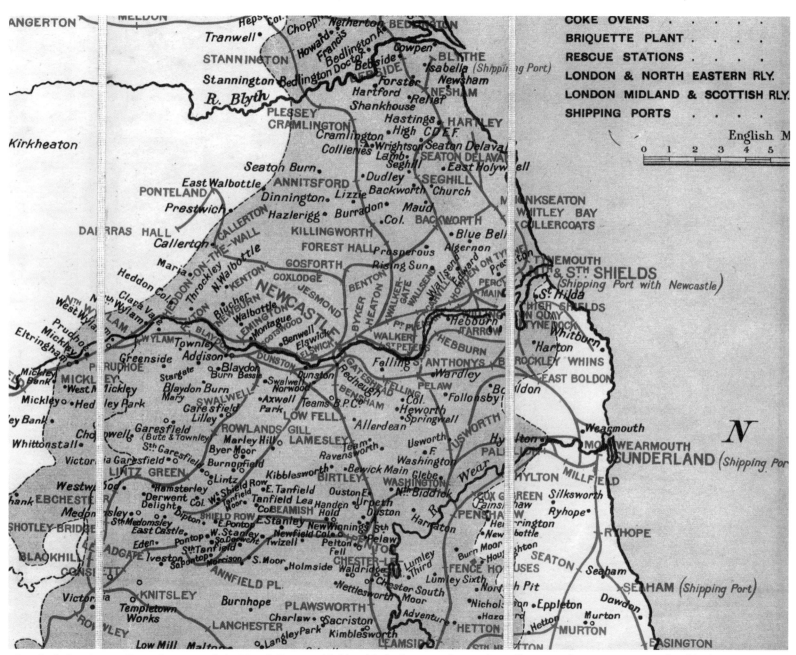

Land of the pitmen. Part of a map of the North East coalfield published in 1900 by Reid's Colliery Guide. Mines are noted in black.

Tunnels beneath Newcastle

There is a tunnel beneath Newcastle city centre which was built to carry coal from the Leazes Main Colliery at Spital Tongues to ships waiting on the Tyne at the mouth of the Ouseburn. Named the Victoria Tunnel, it was constructed in 1839-1842 and runs beneath Claremont Road, the Hancock

Victoria Tunnel, 1939.

Museum site, the grounds of Newcastle Civic Centre, and the Shieldfield district to a point below Byker, close to where the Ouseburn meets the Tyne.

The full waggons used a descending gradient to reach the riverside. The empty waggons were then hauled back up the tunnel by a cable winding engine at the pit. The tunnel has a maximum depth of 85ft and was used as an air raid shelter during the Second World War.

Another tunnel in the Newcastle area was the three-mile long Kitty's Drift, which ran from the East Kenton mine down to staiths on the Tyne at Scotswood. Built in 1796, this passage had a dual role – it was a drain to remove water from the pit and also carried a pony-operated railway for coal waggons.

Loading the coal

Staiths were coal-loading jetties or platforms found at ports and harbours of the North East, including the rivers Tyne and Wear, the harbours of Blyth and Seaham and West Hartlepool Docks. Ships were attended to at the staiths by shore-based workmen known as teemers and trimmers. The teemers carried out the loading of vessels, operating the equipment needed for this. The trimmers, armed with shovels, would level out the coal in the holds, helping to ensure stability and enabling the hatches to be closed. By 1925 there were many staiths on the Tyne, all linked by railways to the pits. One of the most important facilities was Tyne Dock, opened in 1859 on the south bank, which by 1925 had exported more coal than any other dock in the world. By this time steamships had replaced sailing colliers in the trade.

Ten miles up the River Tyne, lay the important Dunston Staiths, opened in 1893. A second set of staiths was added to the facility in 1903. Collier ships would steam up river to Dunston, moving through the opened Swing Bridge.

Dunston Staiths around 1900.

Dunston Staiths

Peter Watson, whose father, David, was shipping superintendent at Dunston Staiths until he retired in the early 70s, has memories of the staiths. Peter writes: 'During school holidays when I was a child in the 1950s I would go and see my father at work some afternoons and walk home with him. I would sit next to him in his office and he would show me how the amount of coal that had to go on to each ship was calculated, where it had come from and where it was going.

'Sometimes I would accompany him when he had to go on to the staiths. It was dirty and noisy, and how hard the teemers and trimmers had to work had to be seen to be believed. The teemers would open the base of the coal trucks to let the coal run down the chutes into the ships. In winter, the fastenings would be frozen and I remember one time seeing them light a fire under a truck to release it. The trimmers would then get to work in the hold, levelling off the coal with shovels and filling in the gaps to ensure the ship would be stable.

Monument to the booming coal trade. Dunston Staiths pictured in 2007. They loaded their last coal shipment in March 1980.

'As a boy one of the highlights for me was when my father would get one of the engine drivers to let me ride the footplate as the engine pulled a seemingly never-ending line of trucks on to the staiths.'

Dunston Staiths, which loaded their last coal shipment in March 1980, still survive today, although a section was destroyed by fire in November 2003. Total coal and coke shipments from the Tyne had reached their peak in 1913 when over 20 million tons was loaded and in 1923 when the figure exceeded 21 million tons.

Thomas Hair's watercolour of a shaft bottom at Walbottle Colliery's Coronation Pit in the 1840s. The glow at the top of the picture is from a burning flare. Corves of coal are seen on a rolley and a corve is being raised up the shaft on a chain.

Lads in the Darkness

'Trapper: A little boy whose employment consists in opening and shutting a trapdoor when required.'

The men who toiled at the coalface in the 18th and 19th centuries were known as hewers. They mined the coal by using their picks to undercut it, then dislodged it from the face manually. More commonly, after 1820, it was blasted down or loose with gunpowder, following undercutting, and broken up where necessary before being loaded into corves and, from the 1840s onwards, into tubs.

The hewer applied his pick to the natural line of breakage in the coal, known as the cleat. To enable him to lie on his side as he undercut the jud (the section of coal to be extracted) he used a small wooden stool, known as a cracket, to support his shoulder. The cracket was also used to support him in a sitting or kneeling position.

Manual undercutting of the coal, an arduous job, was not completely superseded until the widespread adoption of coal-cutting machines in the 20th century, and this changeover was a gradual process. Undercutting by hand continued well into the 20th century at many pits, particularly in difficult, low places where it was impossible to use a machine, making working conditions extremely unpleasant for the miner.

The hewers were the most valued of the mine workers and were paid according to the amount of coal they could win each day. This meant that a hewer was paid per number

Two hewers working coal in a narrow seam, taken from a lantern slide.

Beamish Photographic Archive

of tubs filled, calculated on the basis of a score of tubs. A score varied according to the district, but was 20 or 21. Each man attached a token or tally with a number to his tub to indicate that it was his. A similar system had operated with corves.

Another class of miner was the stoneman. These workers were responsible for excavating the tunnels in a pit, known to miners as headings and roadways, thus advancing the workings. They blasted through rock – hence the name stonemen – and were generally paid by the yardstick, which measured the amounts of stone they removed. In the 20th century tape measures were often employed for this purpose.

During the 19th century North East pits were worked by the bord and pillar method of extraction, sometimes also known as stall and pillar or pillar and wall. This involved mining the coal by means of short tunnels (headings) driven into the seams in criss-cross, interconnecting fashion, leaving pillars of coal in between them to support the roof. Eventually the pillars of coal would also be extracted, leaving a waste area known as the goaf in which the roof collapsed.

However, in the 20th century bord and pillar gradually gave way to the longwall system in which two headings – known as the main gate and tail gate – were driven into a seam parallel to one another, but a considerable distance apart. Then another heading was driven at right angles to connect them and this became the coal face. As the coal was extracted the face advanced and the main gate and tail gate were accordingly moved forward. The coal was removed via the main gate (sometimes called the mothergate), with equipment brought in through the tail. The area behind the coalface was filled with the waste and the roof was collapsed. It was always important that this collapse was thoroughly done, for methane could accumulate if cavities were left.

Despite the trend towards longwall working, many pits in the North East retained the bord and pillar method until their closure. Indeed, several of the mechanised collieries of the late 20th century had both longwall and bord and pillar

Beamish Photographic Archive

Opencasting at Stoney Heap Surface Mine in 2006 reveals bord and pillar workings at Eden Colliery, worked in the 1880s.

systems in operation at the same time in different seams, the older method of bord and pillar by this time being worked with Continuous Miner machines. The method adopted depended upon the nature of the seam.

During the 1700s and early 1800s, the coal was loaded into wicker baskets known as corves (or corfs) for the journey to the surface. The corves were moved along the narrow, often low, tunnels by the putters, who were, more often than not, the sons of hewers. These boys, who started at the age of 9 or 10 and continued until the age of perhaps 19 or 20 when they generally became hewers, pushed and

An illustration from Matthias Dunn's technical manual of 1848, 'The Winning and Working of Collieries', showing putters pulling and pushing a corve.

Boys pull and push a waggon on rails (from Matthias Dunn).

G.C. Greenwell in his Glossary of terms, 1888, describes: 'Headsman: – A lad not strong enough to put alone, but able to do so with the assistance of a little boy, who performs his part by pulling a tub by a couple of ropes or traces attached thereto, called soams. The little boy is called a foal'. He adds that the pay for a 12 hour day for a foal was around one shilling in 1849.

heaved the corves on sledges and in later years on small trolleys with wheels known as trams to the roadways where pony-power could take over. The job required every ounce of their physical strength and was extremely arduous.

Two lads might be employed to move the trams together, the smaller boy being known as a foal. He pulled the tram by means of a rope while the stronger lad, known as a headsman, would push it. Two lads of the same age working as putters were known as half marras. However, older boys in their mid or late teens were often strong enough to move the trams on their own.

Lads of all ages suffered greatly, particularly in low tunnels where their backs would be grazed and cut by the roofs. Injuries were common.

Their long hours of work rendered them utterly exhausted. Many were so tired they wanted to go to sleep as soon as they had eaten their meal after reaching home. In the early 19th century, 12 hours seems to have been the shortest

shift and it is said that many worked shifts lasting up to 17 or 18 hours. They had little or no time for leisure and no chance of going to school. Their employers were happy to keep miners and their families in ignorance of the world at large in case they should get ideas 'above their station'.

The putters pushed and dragged the sledges or trams to landings – assembly points – where the corves could be loaded on to rolleys (larger trams) which ran on rails and were pulled by ponies along the main roadways. It seems that by the early 19th century a considerable number of mines were using small cranes to lift the corves onto the rolleys.

The roadways, or rolleyways as they were generally called, linked up to the shaft bottom from where the corves were raised on a chain or rope to bank – the surface area around the top of the shaft.

As the 19th century progressed, many collieries introduced 'endless' wire rope haulage systems operated by stationary engines to move coal along the roadways. This eventually became the commonest system.

The containers for the coal also changed. By the mid-1840s corves were becoming a thing of the past and most North East pits were converting to tubs for transport. Tubs were small, box-like rail waggons which could be run from the coalface to the landing where they would be linked together in trains, known as sets. From this point they were taken along the main roadways by rail to the foot of the shaft using wire rope haulage or ponies.

Putters – who were paid like the hewers by the number of full tubs delivered at bank with their token attached – would still have to push the tubs to the pony-powered or rope-hauled roadways. However, by the mid-1850s ponies were frequently employed to move the coal from the face to the roadways where conditions were suitable. The younger boys tended to work as drivers and were known appropriately as pony putters. They sat upon the limbers – the shafts attaching the ponies to the tubs. Yet hand-putting continued where the workings were too low for ponies and lasted into the 20th century at some pits.

Once at the shaft bottom the tubs were put into a cage for winding to bank. The first North East colliery to operate a cage may have been Woodside Glebe Pit at Ryton in 1835. This development was a significant advance in safety terms. In the 1700s and into the early 1800s men and boys had been raised and lowered to and from work on the shaft chain or rope. Alternatively they might travel in a corve or some other basket. Clinging to a chain or rope for a descent or ascent of hundreds of feet was, of course, a highly dangerous practice.

In his work *A History of the Parish of Wallsend* (1923), local historian William Richardson describes a particularly sad incident at one of the pits in North Tyneside, said to have been witnessed by Joseph Skipsey, the pitman poet: 'A boy was returning up the shaft clinging to a chain, with his older brother just below him. The youngster felt the chain slowly slipping through his hands. He called out "I'm gannen to fall, Jimmy." "Slide down to me, hinny," his brother replied. But when the boy slid down his brother could not hold him. In spite of an agonising struggle the chain slowly slipped through his fingers, and together they went to their death.'

On another occasion at the same colliery a boy was reported to have fallen asleep with his arms clasped around a rope as he was lowered down the shaft. He was raised again and found to be still asleep when he reached the surface. The tired state of this youngster is telling evidence of long hours of hard labour.

The introduction of tubs meant that cages were needed in the shafts and this ended the highly dangerous practice of using a rope or chain. Now men and boys could travel up and down the shaft in the much greater safety of a cage, which was held in place by wooden or metal guides. Rails were laid in the floor of cages to carry the tubs.

Even though putters started at nine or 10 years upwards,

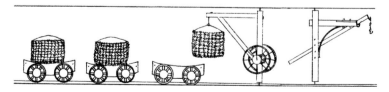

A primitive crane for loading the corves on to rolleys.

they were not the youngest boys to work in the region's mines in the early 1800s. These were the little trapper lads who were generally employed at the ages of six, seven or eight. They were forced to sit for many hours in darkness, operating the trap doors vital to safe ventilation. Instances were recorded of boys as young as five being employed as trappers and there is one report of a youngster going down a pit in the region at the age of four-and-a-half.

This work involved opening the doors every time corves or tubs were moved past. If a boy fell asleep or was distracted from work during one of his long shifts, which lasted 12 or more hours, a door might be left open, and this could result in a firedamp explosion.

An ostensible improvement came in 1842 when legislation banned the employment of boys under the age of 10 underground, but it seems the law was regularly broken. No effective system of mine inspection was put in place to enforce it since only one inspector was appointed and he encountered hostility from coal owners and managers. His powers were very limited. However, an important step forward came in 1850 with the appointment of four new inspectors. Less than a decade later their number had grown to double figures.

It is to the credit of the North East region that no women or girls were employed underground in the region in the 19th century, although they had been until the late 18th century and were employed during the early 19th century in other coalfields of Britain. The Act of 1842 banned them from working underground throughout the country.

W. Fordyce's History of Coal, Coke, Coalfields, 1860, alters one of Thomas Hair's illustrations from 20 years earlier to show wheeled tubs and a cage. Compare the tubs to those in the original watercolour on page 16.

Beamish Photographic Archive

An old roadway associated with Eden Colliery is revealed by opencast workings at Stoney Heap Surface Mine, 2006.

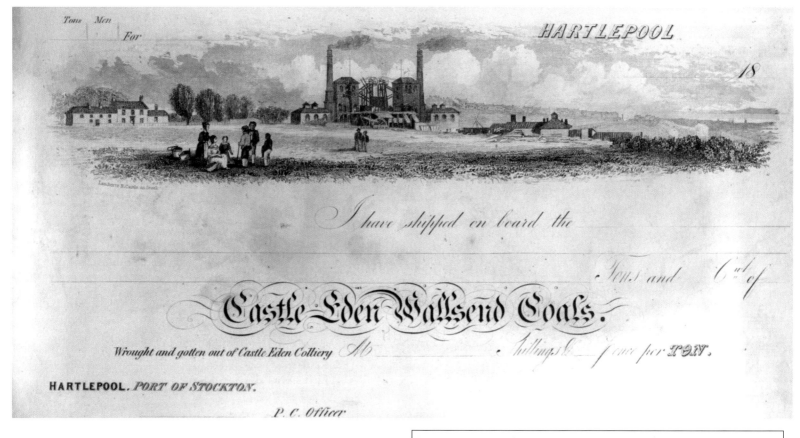

Tons Men

For

HARTLEPOOL

18

I have shipped on board the

Castle Eden Wallsend Coals.

Tons and C^{wt} of

Wrought and gotten out of Castle Eden Colliery At shillings & pence per TON.

HARTLEPOOL. *PORT OF STOCKTON.*

P. C. Officer

Coal certificates were issued by the coal company selling coal and guaranteed the quantity and quality of the product.

The coal from Wallsend pits was judged the best quality. Thomas Hair comments: 'The designation "Wallsend Coal" has continued for many years ... a passport to the quickest sale and the highest prices'. Other mining areas often used the label to their own advantage as here in this certificate from Castle Eden Colliery. The coal certificates from the first half of the 19th century often have detailed and beautifully executed engravings which illustrate mines, coaldrops, and other local scenes.

The Pease Collection at Newcastle Libraries includes a fine collection of coal certificates.

PRICES OF COALS:

Delivered to any part of Newcastle, warranted free from dirt, and weight guaranteed.

PER LOAD OF 15 CWT.

	Near Depot.	Centre.	Any Part.
Lady Windsor's best selected	5 6	5 9	6 0
Original Tanfield's Wallsend	5 6	5 9	6 0
Marley Hill Main Coal	4 6	4 9	5 0
Clavering's Main Do.	4 6	4 9	5 0
Thirds of superior quality	3 9	4 0	4 3

Above: coal prices of Joseph Liddell, coke, coal, and iron merchant of Scotswood Road, Newcastle, from Ward's Directory for 1850. His coal came from Tanfield in County Durham but was still 'Wallsend' quality.

WIDEOPEN COLLIERY.

Thomas Hair (c1810-1875) was a Newcastle-born painter and engraver specialising in landscape and maritime scenes. Between about 1828 and 1842 he produced a series of watercolour sketches, several of which are included in this book. They were preparatory sketches for his books Sketches of the Coal Mines of Northumberland and Durham (1839) and Views of the Collieries of Northumberland and Durham (1842). This engraving by Hair shows Wideopen Colliery which was sunk in 1825. The waggons were unusual here, holding only half a chaldron and being rectangular (also the case at Fawdon). The railway went all the way to the Tyne at Percy Main (about 10 miles). The screens were covered in at this modern pit for the protection of the men and boys, and it was lit at night by gas – a 'neat' gasometer was constructed near the pit.

The Bond

'Bond: The agreement to hire between coalowners and workmen.'

'All these disorders … are only the natural result of the policy of repression which has often been pursued by the authorities in dealing with working men's associations'
Thomas Burt, Northumberland miners' leader

The miners of the North East during the 18th and early 19th centuries lived in conditions of near slavery. They were not truly free men for they were required to sign an annual contract known as the Bond which forced them by law to work for the pit owner for a year. Despite this, the owner had no obligation to give them work during that year.

If they absconded from their employment while under the Bond they could be sentenced by a magistrate to between one and three months imprisonment. Any man who ran away from a pit to find alternative work in the area was almost certainly doomed to disappointment. Other businesses, including mines, were forbidden by law from employing him. If they did so they could be fined £5, a considerable sum in those days.

The power to send miners to jail was not, however, always used. Often a colliery owner might allow a man to return to his work and fine him according to the length of time he had been absent. This could mean he was forced to work for days or weeks without pay. Not unnaturally, the Bond system came to be detested by the miners. This hated contract generally made provision for deducting money from

men should they produce a corve or tub of coal deemed unsatisfactory by the management, opening up scope for unscrupulous employers to deprive men unfairly of money.

Added to these problems was the fact that pitmen and their families lived in rows of cottages owned by their employers and this made them vulnerable to eviction when disputes arose or if they were sacked. Widows of miners were at risk of eviction too.

The coal owners provoked a strike in 1809 when they ruled that the month of the annual signing-on for the Bond would be changed from October to late December or early January. The pitmen took exception to this. They would be forced to accept their pay rate and conditions at a time when work was scarce and this might well drive down wages. A meeting of the men was called at Longbenton in October 1810 and they decided to strike.

Oppressive measures were taken against the strikers, with many of them ending up in Durham Gaol or in a temporary prison – the Bishop of Durham offered his stables for the purpose. Nearly 300 men were locked up in these stables and guarded by soldiers. However, the owners and magistrates did not succeed in breaking the strike and, after a stoppage lasting seven weeks, the miners secured a deal in which a new binding month of April was agreed.

In c1825 a union known as the Colliers' United Association of Durham and Northumberland was formed following the repeal of the Combination Laws which had

North of England Institute of Mining and Mechanical Engineers WKS-11-1

the Persons and Parties herein hired and bound as aforesaid they do and every of them doth bind themselves respectively to the said George Knowsley and William Chapman their Executors Administrators and assigns in the Penal Sum of Fifty Pounds of lawful Money of Great Britain firmly by these Presents, And for the true performance of such Covenants and agreements by such of the said Parties hereby retained and Bound as are Minors their respective Fathers being also parties to these Presents do each and every of them doth bind themselves and himself respectively to the said George Knowsley and William Chapman their Executors Administrators and assigns to do and perform all and every the Conditions covenants and agreements and Work at the Rates and Prices as mentioned and agreed and as more fully explained and particularized in the Bond annexed dated the Seventeenth Day of October in the Year of our Lord One Thousand eight Hundred and Nine —

In Witness whereof the said Parties to these presents have hereunto set their Hands ☛ or Marks and Seals this twenty first day of January in the year of our Lord One Thousand Eight Hundred and ten —

For the Owners of Kenton & Coxlodge Collieries

Thos. Hewitt

No.	Hewers	No.	Hewers	No.	Hewers	No.	Hewers
1	Robert his mark Hall	39	John Cram x his Mark	76	William Young his mark		
2	Patrick x Ramshaw	40	Henry x Bolam	77	Thomas Young his mark		
3	Thomas x Burkham	41	William his mark Middlemas	78	John Brown his mark		
5	Matthew x Bates	42	John Ramsey x his Mark	79	Thomas Coulson x mark		
6	John his mark Bates	43	Christopher Crawford his mark	80	Michael Chapman x		
7	Thomas x Thompson	44	Thomas Crawford x his mark	81	John Joblin — mark		
8	John his mark Hall (Coxlodge)	45	William Brown his mark	82	Joseph Wall — his mark		
9	Robert his mark Hunter	46	John Ramsey his mark	83	John Stoker his mark		
10	John his mark Hall (Slatford)	47	Edward Grunwell mark	84	Nichs. Stoker his mark		
11	William his mark Howey	48	John Peall his mark	85	William x Parkin mark		
12	William x Morton mark	49	John Hall his mark	86	William Watson x mark his		
13							

This Bond document (around 60% of actual size) is from Kenton and Coxlodge pits, 1809-10. There are many more names on the other side of the document. Nearly all the pitmen have signed the contract with their 'mark', generally a cross, because they are unable to write their name.

made unions illegal. The association built up a reported membership of around 4,000. It issued two pamphlets which detailed the men's grievances. A strike was called in 1826 against the Bond, low wages, heavy fines and other poor conditions, but it ended in defeat after seven weeks.

In 1830 a miners' leader emerged who was to head two of the most dramatic early strikes of the North East coalfield. He was Thomas Hepburn, who had been born at Pelton and began work at the age of eight at Urpeth Colliery after his father was killed in a pit accident. Later he worked as a miner at several other collieries, including Fatfield, Jarrow and Hetton. Hepburn led a newly-formed miners' trade union, generally known at the Pitmen's Union of the Tyne and Wear or 'Hepburn's Union'. A Primitive Methodist preacher, he was well suited for this role. This brave man is acknowledged as the leading pioneer of trade unionism in the Great Northern Coalfield.

In March 1831 Hepburn's union organised a mass meeting, attended by 20,000 miners, on the Town Moor in Newcastle. Men from both the Northumberland and County Durham pits came to this great gathering and they paraded through the centre of Newcastle before marching to the Town Moor.

Those at the meeting demanded a reduction in the long working hours, particularly for boys, and an end to the tommy shop system. Tommy shops were stores owned or favoured by employers. They were often run by a relative of the viewer (manager). The men and their families were forced to buy food and provisions from them and money was

THOMAS HEPBURN.

deducted from their wages to pay for these items. The meeting passed a resolution to boycott the shops. It was also agreed that the men should not enter into a new Bond, but instead would continue to work at the pits, unbound, if their employers would let them. If not, they would cease working.

The resulting strike was a bitter one. It began in April, the month of the new binding. After a week or two some miners drifted back to work under the old conditions, but a considerable number of those still on strike attacked machinery and forced pits to close temporarily again. Miners visited collieries in the Blyth and Bedlington district, threatening to set fire to them. At Bedlington Glebe Pit, strikers damaged corves and hurled them down the shaft. Jesmond Dene Colliery in Newcastle was also attacked, with machinery damaged and tipped down the shaft. Men working below were placed in danger by these actions. The same pattern was repeated at Hebburn Colliery, on the southern side of the Tyne, where corves, rolleys and other items were thrown down the pit.

The authorities were swift to act. Marines were drafted into the Tyneside area from Portsmouth, and the Militia, a local force of soldiers, as well as regular troops, were called out. They guarded pits or patrolled the streets of the mining villages. For example, at pits in the Wallsend area a number of men who had returned to work were given protection by the soldiers, who also kept watch over the machinery. Hetton Colliery in County Durham seems to have been regarded as a particular hotbed of discontent. Infantry soldiers from Sunderland Barracks guarded the mine and village.

On April 21 1831, the striking pitmen held a mass

meeting at Jarrow. The banners of each colliery were paraded in a show of solidarity and the pitmen's leaders urged their members to remain orderly and conduct themselves in a peaceful way. There was clearly a need for such an appeal, given the incidents of the previous days. Hepburn was aware of the need to rein in those men whose actions might discredit their cause.

In early May, the miners again assembled, this time on Black Fell, near Washington. They must have been astonished when they saw the powerful County Durham coal owner, the 3rd Marquess of Londonderry, arrive with an escort of soldiers and accompanied by magistrates. He asked the men to disperse on penalty of the Riot Act being read and pledged to meet their representatives in Newcastle for talks. The men agreed to the request and the open-air meeting ended peacefully.

The men went on to win a partial victory. The strike ended in mid-June after the owners agreed to a number of points,

North of England Institute of Mining and Mechanical Engineers Wat 1-28-7

THE PITMEN.

TO THE PUBLIC.

From the PITMEN of the Tyne and Wear.

MEETING of DELEGATES, *Newcastle, 28th. April, 1831*.

THIS IS TO CERTIFY, to the Public at large, that we proposed to meet the Coal-Owners to-day, agreeably to their wish, and accordingly waited upon them, in order to discuss the Differences unhappily existing between them and us : but they have positively thrown Contempt upon our offer, and have refused to meet us ; in consequence, we are obliged to return Home again without doing any Business.

We would here observe to the Owners, that we wish them not to be misled by their Agents, for we are determined to have our reasonable Requests, which are as follow :——

I. Not to be turned out of our Houses at the Expiration of our Hiring, according to our Bond, but to let the Law have its regular Process.

II. We wish to have Eleven Days per Fortnight, at Three Shillings per Day, which will leave about Twenty-nine Shillings, after every Deduction.

III. The Time of Working to be henceforth Twelve Hours per Day.

IV. Fines for laid-out Corves to be only the Loss of the Price of the Corf ; and Corves deficient in Measure to be set out at the Crane.

V. Corves to be adjusted when thought to be too large.

VI. The annual Binding to be at the usual Time.

Newcastle : MARSHALL, Printer.

including two of their key demands. The working shift for boys was cut to 12 hours and the men were allowed to buy provisions from whatever store they chose. To what extent this agreement was honoured is hard to ascertain. But the Bond system remained in place. The first employer to make the concessions had been the Marquess of Londonderry – but only because he was financially stretched by his scheme to build a harbour at Seaham for coal shipments.

It was a victory for the men, but the employers, not least of them Lord Londonderry, had been perturbed by the development of trade unionism in the mines. They were determined to crush Hepburn's Union, as it was popularly known, and when the date of the 1832 binding arrived union members were refused work. It was, of course, a recipe for continued trouble. Other miners, supporting their comrades, refused to sign the Bond.

At a mass meeting on Boldon Fell in early March 1832, the men again demonstrated their solidarity. Richard Fynes, in his classic work *The Miners of Northumberland and Durham* (1873) writes of this great gathering: 'The men began to arrive from their respective collieries shortly after 9 o'clock in the morning and by 11 o'clock there was an immense number on the ground, the men from each colliery bringing with them banners bearing various mottoes and devices.'

The pitmen duly went on strike, refusing to sign the Bond. The owners responded by evicting miners who were union members and their families from tied cottages. This was often done under the supervision of special constables and could lead to violence. Men from other parts of Britain, including Wales and Ireland and lead miners from the North Pennines, were then brought in as blackleg labour and housed in the cottages. It is likely that many were unaware of the dispute when they were signed on.

At Hetton, it was reported that union men were rounded up by special constables and locked in stables all night, bound hand and foot. Any miners congregating in groups were regarded as potential troublemakers or malcontents and arrested.

Tom Yellowley

The 3rd Marquess of Londonderry, a strong opponent of the miners' trade unions. This famed equestrian statue of the coal owner stands in Durham City Market Place.

At Friars Goose Colliery, on the banks of the Tyne in Gateshead, there was a major clash between pitmen and constables during evictions. The officers had been issued with loaded pistols and a number of the miners managed to capture some of these weapons. The policemen were on the receiving end of volleys of stones and other missiles and shots were fired on both sides. Up to six constables were reportedly wounded as a result of the disturbance, although at least one account suggests that six pitmen were the casualties. At Fawdon, troops were called in to assist police as the pitmen vowed 'they would die to a man before their furniture should be removed'. In another incident, John Herrington, a Hetton miner who had been among the few to return to work, was shot dead.

Feelings were understandably running very high and in June 1832 magistrate Nicholas Fairless, of South Shields, was pulled off his horse on the outskirts of the town. He was attacked and received fatal injuries. Two men were alleged to have been involved in this crime, Ralph Armstrong and William Jobling. Armstrong escaped, but Jobling, a miner, was accused of the murder, put on trial, found guilty and hanged at Durham. His body was covered in pitch and hung in an iron frame from a gibbet at Jarrow Slake, close to the scene of the killing. Jobling was one of the last men in England to suffer this gruesome fate. Such a macabre punishment only served to fuel anger further.

Within a month, Jobling's body was taken down from the gibbet. Who carried this out remains a mystery, but it may well have been miners appalled at seeing the body of a

A newspaper depicts the attack upon Nicholas Fairless. There is good reason to believe miner William Jobling was innocent of the crime.

fellow pitman treated with such dreadful indignity, or perhaps Jobling's relatives and friends. After that the body disappeared, but there is some evidence to support the rumour that Jobling's body was buried in the Jarrow area. There is also good reason to believe that this unfortunate man was innocent of the killing.

In July, during an altercation between miners and constables at Chirton, near North Shields, Cuthbert Skipsey, an overman from the nearby Percy Main Colliery who intervened in an attempt to calm the situation, was shot dead by a special constable armed with a pistol. The police officer was sentenced to six months' hard labour for manslaughter. The discrepancy between Jobling's sentence and that received by the constable did not go unnoticed by the miners and their families.

By this time, however, the men were beginning to drift back to work. Thomas Hepburn must have known the cause of trade unionism in the North East pits had suffered a grievous blow, as the returning miners were forced to give up union membership as a condition of employment. Wage reductions followed the strike. Hepburn was refused work at the pits he applied to. Rendered destitute, he is said to have sold tea in the streets. The leader did eventually find a job – at Felling Colliery in Gateshead – but only on condition that he too gave up all union activity.

Twelve years after the 1832 strike another great dispute gripped the Northumberland and Durham coalfield. In 1841-42, another union, the Miners' Association of Great Britain and Ireland, was set up by pitmen in northern England. Among its leading lights was Martin Jude, treasurer of a newly-formed Northumberland and Durham union which was affiliated to the national organisation.

In 1844, the Northumberland and Durham miners led a campaign by the national association to end the Bond system and improve wages and conditions. The resulting strike of that year again led to mass evictions from tied cottages and to importation of blackleg labour from other areas of the country.

County Durham coal and mine owner the 3rd Marquess of Londonderry was a particularly unpopular employer – for good reason. He ordered that no credit be given to striking miners by shopkeepers in Seaham, a place he regarded as his personal possession. The marquess was reported to have attended evictions. His presence did not endear him to the pitmen. Lord Londonderry also fiercely opposed the appointment of mines inspectors.

Richard Fynes tells us that men from both counties held a mass meeting on Shadon's Hill between Wrekenton and Birtley in March 1844. There were said to be at least 20,000 present. Some men had walked between 20 and 30 miles to attend. It must have been an extraordinary spectacle as an 'army' of miners assembled to air their grievances. As well as opposing the yearly Bond, they called for better wages, the weighing of coals and the appointment of mines inspectors to improve ventilation and other aspects of safety. A second meeting took place on the hill the following month when the stoppage began. It was attended by an even larger gathering of pitmen, accompanied by banners and bands.

The Northumberland and Durham miners were the only ones in the country to take strike action on this occasion, but they had the backing of the national association and a pledge that members in other regions would not become blacklegs. Nevertheless, the employers were successful in bringing in blackleg labour.

Fynes writes of the mass evictions of 1844: 'Age and sex were disregarded, no woman was too weak, no child too young, no grandma or grandsire too old; but all must go forth'. He tells his readers that 'wholesale turning to the door commenced at every colliery village'. At Pelton Fell Colliery a blind woman aged 88 was evicted. Two young men with a bedridden mother were also turned out into the street. Among the many others ejected from their homes was a young woman 'expecting to be a mother every hour'. Another woman was 'dragged by the neck 100 yards'.

The outcome of the epic 1844 dispute was something of a surprise. Although after 17 weeks on strike the men went back to work defeated, the annual Bond system was not revived by the employers. Instead, they put in place a monthly Bond in the hope of being able to get rid of union agitators more easily. The leaders of the strike were not re-employed. Wage reductions followed.

The monthly Bond was to last for nearly 20 years, but mine owners found that men and their families were moving from pit to pit after only short spells and this caused them difficulties. Accordingly, the employers announced that from April 1864 they would re-instate the yearly Bond. This move was resisted by the miners and led to a revival of trade unionism in the coalfields. The Northumberland employers dropped the yearly Bond plan as a result of this opposition, but the system survived in County Durham. Not until 1872 was this hated annual contract finally abolished throughout the Great Northern Coalfield.

Thomas Hepburn, clearly a man of great courage and of peaceful intent, believed colliery villages should be provided with libraries so that miners and their children could be educated. He died in 1864 and is buried in St Mary's Churchyard, Heworth, Gateshead, where North East miners pay tribute to him each year at a memorial service. Lodge banners are displayed inside the church for the occasion and wreaths are laid at his graveside.

The inscription on the tomb includes the words: 'Shorter hours and better education for miners.' It also states: 'He initiated the first great union of Northern miners in 1831 and conducted the strike of 1832 with great forbearance and ability. His life was spent in advocating shorter hours of labour and extended education for miners.' Thomas Hepburn Community School at Gateshead is named after this pioneering leader. It is fitting that Hepburn lies at rest on Tyneside at the heart of the Great Northern Coalfield where he fought against virtual slavery and where today people enjoy a standard of living and degree of freedom from the control of their employers unheard of in his time.

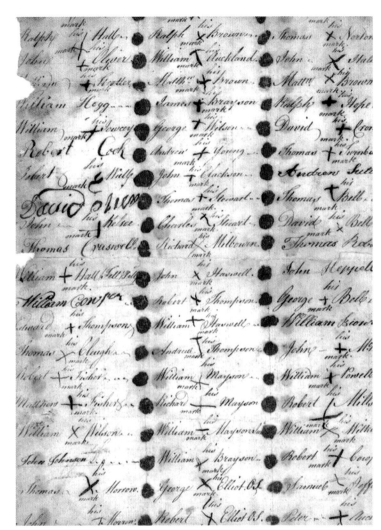

Part of a miners' Bond document from a pit at Walker, dated 1772. Again, many crosses are in evidence.

Tribute to a brave leader – Union pioneer Tommy Hepburn remembered

Ken Smith

The congregation gathers at the graveside of Thomas Hepburn in St Mary's Churchyard, Heworth, Gateshead, during the 2007 annual memorial service.

On the morning of October 13, 2007, St Mary's Churchyard at Heworth is full of miners, their families and friends. They are gathering for the annual tribute to the greatest pioneer of mining trade unionism in the North East.

An advocate of better education for miners, Thomas Hepburn was unable to obtain work in any pit for over two years following the 1832 strike. Victimised, he was reduced to poverty. More than 140 years after his death, the miners are assembling on a grey autumn day to remember this brave man and what he stood for. At least one of them has been coming to the service for 20 years.

Seventeen miners' banners make a colourful backdrop to the service. The oldest is from Thornley – made in the early 1950s. This survivor of many parades depicts the Greenwood Aged Miners' Homes in Thornley. The church is full. The musical accompaniment to the hymns is provided by the majestic brass of the NUM North East Area Band. The address is given by former miner David Hamilton, MP for Midlothian. A group of young people from Thomas Hepburn Community School in Gateshead are also present and one of the girls reads the lesson.

Richard Smith

After the service, the men carry the banners, in procession, to Tommy's graveside in the churchyard. The rest of the congregation follows. Miners' representatives and councillors lay wreaths as the band plays *Gresford*, the pitmen's anthem. Tommy Hepburn is long gone – but he will never be forgotten by the miners.

The wreaths at Hepburn's grave, 2007.

Poet of the Collieries

Joseph Skipsey, the pitman poet in his miner's clothes pictured in Robert Spence Watson's biography.

Joseph Skipsey, the pitman poet, was born at Percy Main, North Tyneside, in 1832. During the great strike of that year Joseph's father, Cuthbert, an overman at Percy Main Colliery, was shot dead by a special constable during a disturbance between strikers and police. Cuthbert had been trying to defuse the situation. The loss of the breadwinner plunged his family into abject poverty. They were said to have lived for a time on nettle broth with an occasional slice of bread.

At the age of seven Joseph began work as a trapper at Percy Main Colliery, sitting for up to 16 hours in darkness. He was carried to and from the pit, part of the way by one of his brothers. Later he became a putter. He taught himself to read and write and at the age of 15 was lent several books by an uncle. It was to prove one of the most important developments of Joseph's life.

At the age of 20 Joseph walked all the way to London to seek an improvement in his position. He did not find it, but while in the capital he met his future wife and brought her home to Tyneside with him. They attempted to run a village school together but this did not provide an adequate living so Joseph returned to mining, this time as a hewer. As well as Percy Main, he was employed for a time at Backworth, Newsham, Cowpen and Ashington collieries.

Robert Spence Watson, a well-known Tyneside solicitor and radical Liberal who admired his work, became the talented pitman's friend. Among Joseph's anthologies were *Poems, Songs & Ballads* (1862), *The Collier Lad and Other Lyrics* (1864), *Carols from the Coalfields* (1886) and *Songs & Lyrics* (1892). Joseph's best known poems include '*Get Up*', *The Hartley Calamity* and *The Collier Lad*. Joseph Skipsey, the laureate of the collieries, passed away in 1903. He is buried in Gateshead Cemetery.

Another pitman poet was Tommy Armstrong, born at Shotley Bridge, County Durham, in 1848. He wrote poems that were set to music, including a well-known one on the Trimdon Grange disaster. He lived much of his life in the Tanfield Lea area. Tommy died in 1920 and is buried in St Margaret's Churchyard, Tanfield village. A new headstone on the grave quotes a poem by Tommy, entitled *Durham Strike* – which includes a tribute to Northumberland miners for their help to Durham pitmen in 1892.

Geordies and Glennies

'A lamp that may be carried with perfect safety into the most explosive atmosphere.'
George Stephenson

In around 1813, Sunderland physician Dr William Reid Clanny devised a 'safety lamp' aimed at giving miners protection from the explosive effects of firedamp. Born in County Down, Ireland, Clanny practised at the Sunderland Infirmary for many years. Despite his good intentions, his first lamp proved impractical.

Within two years other men were tackling the challenge. Killingworth Colliery, like many other mines in the North East, suffered its share of tragedies brought about by the 'fiery' nature of the coal seams. More than 20 were killed as the result of methane explosions at the mine in 1806 and 1809. Locomotive pioneer George Stephenson, enginewright at Killingworth, had personal experience of these tragedies and it is not surprising that he should have brought his mind to bear on the problem. Firedamp bedevilled the workings.

In August 1815 Stephenson began carrying out experiments to devise a safety lamp to protect miners from the gas. Some of these experiments took place down one of the Killingworth Colliery pits and involved carrying lighted candles near 'blowers'. These were fissures in the rock from which the methane (then simply referred to as hydrogen or carburetted hydrogen) issued. Such experiments were, of course, extremely dangerous.

His eventual idea was to surround an oil flame with a protective glass cylinder and to encase this in a tin cylinder. Three versions of the lamp were produced, each one an improvement on the last. In the first version, air was allowed

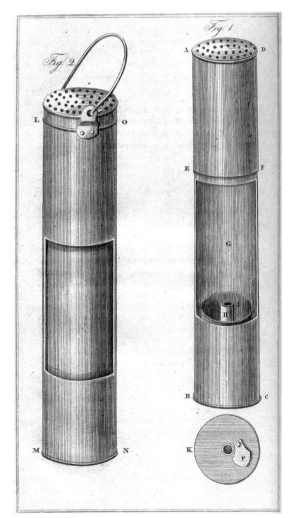

An early design for George Stephenson's safety lamp, known as the Geordie.

to reach the flame by means of a tube at the base of the lamp. In the third version, air was admitted to the tin cylinder and to the top and base of the glass cylinder by numerous small holes.

Meanwhile, in London the nationally famous scientist Sir Humphry Davy was also working on the problem and he too drew up plans for a safety lamp, which by coincidence was identical in principle, though not in form, to Stephenson's. The truth is that both men had developed the same idea independently of one another. However, Stephenson, quite unintentionally, had his lamp in use before Davy's.

Davy announced his plan for a lamp at a meeting of the Royal Society in London in November 1815. The following month, Stephenson demonstrated his lamp, which became known as the Geordie Lamp after its inventor, at a meeting of Newcastle's Literary and Philosophical Society. But, the Stephenson lamp was already in use at Killingworth Colliery. He had had it made by a Newcastle tinsmith and taken it into the mine in late October 1815.

Two years later, Stephenson wrote: 'This lamp was tried in Killingworth Colliery on October 21, 1815. The idea I had long entertained and the drawing was shown to several persons employed in that concern, two months before the day above mentioned, when I carried it with safety into a part of the mine where a strong blower of hydrogen was coming off. An experiment which was immediately repeated in the presence of two persons employed in that concern.'

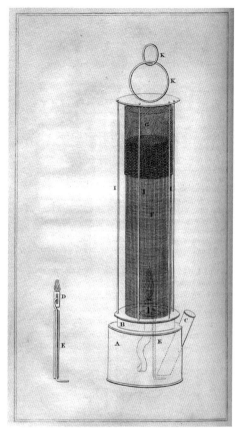

The design for the Davy Lamp.

The two men who accompanied Stephenson into the mine on this momentous occasion were his friend, apprentice viewer Nicholas Wood, and another fellow worker, under-viewer John Moodie. Modern research points strongly to the possibility that Wood contributed ideas towards the lamp.

Stephenson was clearly a man of considerable bravery. The methane could be heard hissing out from a crack in the rock. Indeed, it was said to be coming out more strongly than usual. When Wood and Moodie heard the powerful blower they decided to go no further, but Stephenson pressed onwards. However, before he reached the spot where the gas was issuing from the roof the flame went out. But there was no blast.

He then returned to his companions, re-lit the flame and moved towards the blower for a second time. On reaching it, he held the lamp directly in front of the escaping methane. Again, there was no explosion. Instead, the flame went out, as before.

Stephenson returned once more to Wood and Moodie and he persuaded them to approach closer to the blower. He then repeated the experiment. For a third time, there was no blast. This emboldened Wood, who is believed to have held the lamp in front of the blower himself. All lived to tell the tale.

Despite this success, a furious dispute erupted when Sir Humphry Davy was hailed nationally as the inventor of the safety lamp and awarded £2,000. It was even alleged that

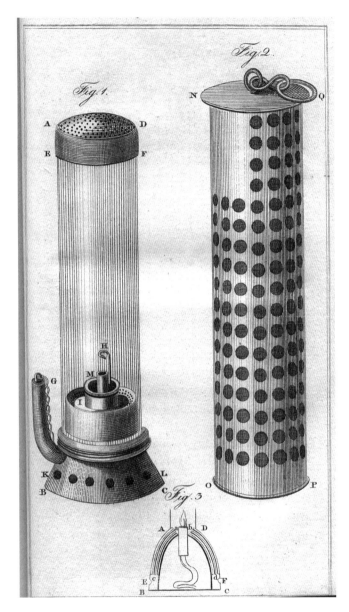

The early Geordie lamp design which was eventually adopted by Killingworth Colliery.

Tom Yellowley

A safety lamp depicted in a stained glass window at Neville Hall, Newcastle.

Stephenson had in some way borrowed Davy's ideas. Stephenson's supporters in the North East were stung by these claims, and were swift to assert that their man had been the real inventor.

North East men of wealth and power, including a leading group of mine owners known as the Grand Allies, another colliery owner, Charles Brandling, and manufacturer William Losh, were stout in their defence of Stephenson. In 1817 a

North East committee of inquiry met at the Assembly Rooms, Newcastle, to look into the issue. Witnesses testified to the committee that Stephenson's lamp was the first in use and his name was cleared of the allegation that he had borrowed Davy's idea.

The committee 'ascertained that as early as August 1815' Stephenson 'was busied with various experiments upon the air proceeding from blowers in coal mines'. The enginewright was accordingly awarded £1,000 and a silver tankard by his supporters. Yet even in the North East there were supporters of Davy, including the prominent viewer John Buddle junior. Davy had tested his lamp at Hebburn Colliery.

The Geordie Lamp was said to have been used by miners in a considerable number of North East pits. The Davy, which was surrounded with a wire gauze, did not have a glass cylinder. Occasionally, a draught might cause the flame from a Davy to pass through the gauze and make contact with gas. The Geordie, with its protective glass cylinder enclosing the flame, did not suffer from this defect.

In addition, the upper part of the Davy was said to have a tendency to become overheated, another potential hazard in gaseous conditions. The Geordie's glass cylinder helped to prevent this happening. However, in c1820 Stephenson re-designed his lamp, surrounding it with a gauze, similar to Davy's, but he retained the vital glass cylinder. Yet the Geordie was not perfect; one of its defects was that it could become dangerous if the glass was broken.

Dr Clanny, the first man to devise a safety lamp, went on

Three miners' lamps: left to right, a Davy Lamp (this type is sometimes called a 'Newcastle-type Davy'); a carbide lamp, probably c1930, as used in mine areas free from gas; and a flame safety lamp of the 20th century.

to develop four more versions of his invention. The last version, brought out in c1842, featured a gauze like Davy's, but the gauze was shorter and below it a large glass cylinder gave a good 'window' for the light.

Other inventors in the 19th century developed improved safety lamps, but they all learned from the basic ideas of Clanny, Stephenson and Davy. Indeed, the Clanny came to be called a 'Glennie' by many of the North East pitmen and as time passed they began using this name for all types of flame safety lamps, even the later, improved ones. However, in some parts of the coalfield the term 'Davy' was used in this way.

Another lamp popular in some North East pits was the carbide. This worked by releasing drops of water from an upper chamber in the lamp into a compartment below containing calcium carbide, thus producing acetylene gas which could be lit. The carbide lamp was therefore a naked flame and only suitable in mine areas free from methane.

It is possible that the term 'Geordie', the name by which people born on Tyneside are affectionately known to this day, originates from the Geordie Lamp's use by some of the Tyneside miners. What is certain, however, is that safety lamps, of whatever type, saved countless men from death.

From the late 1920s and 1930s onwards battery-operated electric cap lamps began to be introduced, although this was a gradual process at first. Very few miners had electric cap lamps before the Second World War. Despite the advent of the electric lamp, flame safety lamps continued to be carried because they were superb gas detectors.

During the 20th century electric lighting was introduced at junctions on main roadways and at shaft bottoms. Electric handlamps were carried by those men working on main roadways. For more about safety lamps see pages 92-93.

From the late 1920s and 1930s onwards electric cap lamps began to be introduced, although this was a gradual process. Very few miners had them before the Second World War. This view of Kibblesworth Colliery lamp cabin shows Oldham electric lamps, c1950s. A miner's electric cap lamp battery would be recharged between his shifts. Flame safety lamps continued to be carried for gas detection.

Whirlwinds of Flaming Air

'Blast: An explosion of fire-damp extending over a great part of the workings of a colliery.'

'Get up!' the caller calls 'get up!'
And in the dead of night,
To win the bairns their bite and sup,
I rise a weary wight.

My flannel dudden donn'd,
Thrice o'er my birds are kissed, and then
I with a whistle shut the door,
I may not ope' again.

              Joseph Skipsey, pitman poet

The 19th century witnessed a mounting death toll from colliery disasters in the North East, the majority caused by firedamp explosions. These tragedies were, in many cases, blamed on the use of candles, naked flame oil lamps or shot-firing. Inadequate ventilation and coal dust were also important factors. Death tolls of between 10 and 50 miners were by no means uncommon. In the worst cases, the number of fatalities reached treble figures.

The Geordie and Davy lamps were of great use in detecting firedamp, but they also emboldened mine owners to send men into areas previously thought too dangerous. In addition, it seems there was a widespread insistence by leading viewers that as candles were needed to light gunpowder fuses, safety lamps should be excluded when blasting, although the logic of this is far from clear. There was always the danger that employers would neglect the need for good ventilation because of over-reliance on the lamps. These pioneering lamps could also be dangerous in some situations, such as over-rapid draughts of air.

Lulled into a false sense of security by the presence of safety lamps, miners would light candles or unprotected oil flames to provide much better illumination than the lamps could give. Alternatively, they might turn the safety lamp flame up very high, possibly causing the gauze to overheat. The temptation was a strong one in the utter blackness of a pit and when a hewer's wages depended on the amount of coal he could win.

The use of candles or naked oil flames – sometimes held in an open-sided metal container to form what was known as a 'midgie' lamp – was seemingly harmless in non-gaseous

A naked flame was a terrible hazard.

areas, but conditions could change rapidly and any sudden manifestation or build-up of firedamp was highly dangerous when naked lights were present, particularly if ventilation was inadequate.

On October 6, 1805, an explosion killed 35 miners at Hebburn Colliery on the south side of the river. Historian M.A. Richardson (1844) tells us that 25 widows and 81 children were left 'unprovided for'. But this was only a portent of the terrible death toll which was to mount throughout the 19th century in the region's pits.

On May 25, 1812, 92 men and boys died as the result of an explosion at Felling Colliery, between central Gateshead and Hebburn. This mine was owned by the influential and wealthy Brandling family of Gosforth Park.

At Felling, the first signs of disaster witnessed on the surface were two blasts and a flame issuing from the downcast shaft, the John Pit, with an immense roar. Shortly afterwards there was a third explosion from the upcast shaft, the William Pit, which was several hundred yards away. This was also accompanied by a flame.

Recovery of 91 bodies took around four months and one miner was never found. The youngest of those who died were two trapper boys aged eight. Three injured boys who were brought to the surface passed away within a few hours of the disaster. Most of the 28 putters who lost their lives were in their teens. Also among the dead were 34 hewers and a deputy. The miners had been working in the newly opened Low Main Seam, the High Main having been exhausted the year before.

An old postcard shows the John Pit at Felling Colliery in 1933. More than 100 years earlier, an explosion at this mine killed 92 men and boys.

A grim depiction of the aftermath of the Felling disaster from a contemporary pamphlet.

The Rev John Hodgson, of nearby Heworth, conducted the funeral service for the 92 victims and afterwards wrote a detailed account of the accident and its aftermath, entitled *Funeral Sermon* and published in 1813. It must have made uneasy reading for the Brandlings and other mine owners.

Hodgson told his readers that in such explosions 'the whole mine is instantly illuminated with the most brilliant lightning – the expanded fluid drives before it a roaring whirlwind of flaming air which tears up everything in its progress, scorching some of the miners to a cinder, burying others under enormous heaps of ruins shaken from the roof, and, thundering to the shafts, wastes its volcanic fury in a discharge of thick clouds of coal dust, stones, timber, and not infrequently limbs of men and horses'.

Hodgson wrote of the dust which was blown out from the Felling shafts: 'The heaviest part of the ejected matter, such as corves, pieces of wood and small coal, fell near the pits, but the dust, borne away by a strong west wind, fell in a continued shower from the pit to the distance of a mile and a half. In the village of Heworth it caused a darkness like that of early twilight, and covered the roads so thickly that the footsteps of passengers were strongly imprinted upon it.'

He reported: 'As soon as the explosions were heard, the wives and children of the workmen ran to the pit. Wildness and terror was pictured in every countenance. The crowd from all sides soon collected to the number of several hundred, some crying out for a husband, others for a father or son … '

Mineworkers with their horse pose for a picture at the John Pit of Felling Colliery, c1890. A chaldron-style waggon is behind them.

Hodgson's detailed account of the Felling tragedy led to the establishment of the Society for the Prevention of Accidents in Mines, based in Sunderland. Backed by a number of influential figures, including mine owners such as the Brandlings, the society was able to call upon the services of Sir Humphry Davy to look into the possibility of developing a safety lamp. As we have seen, Davy visited the North East to carry out experiments at about the same time as George Stephenson was experimenting to devise his lamp. It was all too late for the Felling victims.

Their memorial can be found in St Mary's Churchyard, Heworth, close to Heworth Metro Station. It is a small

91 PERSONS KILLED

JOHN. A. DOBSON. AGED	13.
ROBERT DOBSON	13.
DOBSON	
PAUL FLETCHER	22
WILL : GALLEY	22.
GREG : GALLEY	10.
MICH : GARDINER	45.
WILL : GARDINER	10.
ROBERT GORDON	40.
JOSEPH GORDON	10.
THOMAS GORDON	8.
ISAAC GREENER	65.
ISAAC GREENER	24.
JOHN GREENER	21.
RALPH HALL	18.
ROBERT HALL	13.
RA : HARRISON	39.
ROB : HARRISON	14.
JOHN HARRISON	12.
ROB : HASWELL	42.
JOHN HASWELL	22.
EDW : HASWELL	20.
HEN : HASWELL	18.

A plaque on the Felling disaster memorial at St Mary's Churchyard, Heworth, lists victims and their ages. Often, several members of a family have been lost.

obelisk with brass plaques on four sides listing the names of the dead. The memorial stands by a section of the churchyard wall, close to the road and near one of the entrance gates.

Three years after Felling came a tragedy which had

nothing to do with firedamp. The accident occurred at Heaton Main Colliery between the centre of Newcastle and Wallsend on May 3, 1815, when 75 men and boys were killed by an inrush of water from old workings. Two pitmen encountered the water as they carried out boring to extend a drift tunnel. Worried by the sudden flooding, they told a boy to run and warn the other miners of the danger. He was to advise everyone to head for the shaft and escape.

The lad, who may have been very young, started off on his errand, but the talk of the men about the danger and the gushing of the water had frightened him. He was alone and in darkness without any company. Instead he hurried to the shaft and was drawn to bank. Meanwhile, the inrush of water increased and developed into an unstoppable flood. An engineer, William Miller, tried to warn the men to head for the surface, but he lost his life as he was engulfed by the water which soon filled up the area around the bottom of the shaft, blocking the miners' only way of escape.

A total of 41 men and 34 boys were now trapped underground in part of the Heaton workings which remained clear of water. Would-be rescuers tried to reach them by using old shafts, but without success. It was nine months before the bodies of these 75 tragic miners were recovered. They were found to be high above the water level and had been forced to slaughter a pony for food. The water which caused the disaster had burst in from disused workings of the older Heaton and Jesmond collieries which had been abandoned in the 18th century.

Barely a month later, on June 2, 1815, a disaster with an all too familiar cause hit the Success Pit, Newbottle, to the north of Houghton-le-Spring. Here, an explosion led to the deaths of 57 miners. Some of the casualties were overcome by afterdamp.

The cost in human lives of winning the coal rose still further. On October 23, 1821, 52 men and boys were killed in a firedamp explosion at Wallsend Colliery. It was not the first such blast at this mine, but it was the most serious accident at the colliery to that date. According to historian William Richardson (1923) the power of the explosion shook the ground above and made the furniture and crockery in the houses 'dance'. Only four of the 56 men and boys who were down the pit survived.

At Wallsend the High Main seam had been virtually exhausted by 1831 and afterwards the coal was mined from another, deeper seam, the Bensham. This seam was particularly fiery, presenting the pitmen with the constant danger of firedamp. Its hazardous nature was demonstrated to appalling effect on June 18, 1835, when 102 men and boys from the town were killed as the result of a firedamp explosion. Many seem to have died from the afterdamp (carbon monoxide) or chokedamp (a high level of carbon dioxide and low level of oxygen) occurring in the wake of the blast. Other bodies were found with burns or crush injuries.

Among the dead was an adult miner surrounded by a group of boys. The man had evidently been trying to lead the boys to safety towards the nearest shaft, the G Pit, although had they succeeded in reaching it they would have found it blocked by the explosion. Poignantly, each lad was discovered with his cap in his mouth in a bid to combat the effects of the afterdamp.

Few, if any of the rows of pitmen's

cottages in Wallsend were untouched by this great tragedy. Everyone knew or was related to at least one victim. The two youngest boys killed were aged eight and nine. Several others were only 11 or 12. The oldest miner, incredibly, was aged 76. The dead were given a last resting place in the town's St Peter's Churchyard, not far from the G-pit, which was also known as the Church Pit. Sadly, the mass grave was unmarked. There was no memorial for these men and boys.

Thirty-nine of the miners who died in the Heaton flooding disaster had been given a memorial plaque at St Peter's, which is still sited inside the church. They too are buried in the churchyard. Many Wallsend men and boys had worked at the Heaton colliery. It seemed illogical and unfair that the 102 who lost their lives in the Wallsend Colliery

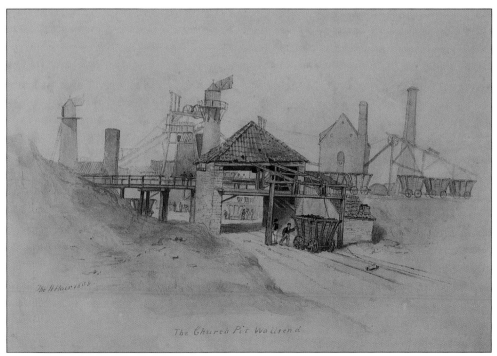

Collection of the Hatton Gallery, Newcastle University

Thomas Hair's watercolour of the Church Pit (G Pit) of Wallsend Colliery.

explosion should not have a memorial too. This situation was at last rectified in 1994 when a commemorative plaque was sited on the inner south wall of the churchyard. This was made possible thanks to the efforts of Wallsend Local History Society in combination with the National Union of Mineworkers and North Tyneside Council.

On August 3, 1830, 42 miners were killed at Jarrow Colliery. An explosion took place in the Bensham seam, the same band of coal which was to prove so disastrous on the north side of the river at Wallsend. It was said the Jarrow men had accidentally broken into old workings from which firedamp had issued and that it was possible the accident had been caused by 'negligence in the use of the Davy lamp'. Whether this was through use of candles, failure to use a safety lamp or some defect in the lamp, such as damage or detachment of the gauze, does not seem to have been made clear. The *Newcastle Courant* reported that 21 of the men killed had left widows and a total of 66 children. Ten miners had been badly injured.

Jarrow local historian Jim Cuthbert, of Fellgate, writes: 'A newspaper report of the 1830 disaster drew public attention to the fact that there was no relief fund organised to support the widows and their children, not to mention those injured in the explosion. However, George Major, a prominent Monkton landowner, organised a relief committee, which raised £932.15s.6d. This money came from throughout the North East coalfield. The owners of the Jarrow pit subscribed £50, which was less than £1 per man or boy killed or maimed.'

Jim believes the families of the dead miners would have been evicted from their pit cottages in Jarrow to allow newcomers to replace them. He is likely to be right, as this was the usual course of action taken by owners.

On May 9, 1833, 47 lives were extinguished by a blast at Springwell Colliery, to the south of Gateshead.

The St Hilda Colliery, South Shields, suffered a major disaster on June 28, 1839, when 51 men and boys died as the result of yet another devastating firedamp explosion. This was another Brandling family colliery. The workings had hitherto been considered safe and candles and blasting with gunpowder were regularly used.

On the day of the disaster smoke mixed with small coals exploded from the downcast shaft and soon afterwards about 100 men and boys were brought to bank. Some were suffering from the effects of chokedamp. A large crowd gathered at the pithead.

A number of men descended the shaft again to try to rescue their fellow miners, but they found only bodies. It was reported that efforts to find anyone who might be alive and recover the dead were hampered by the chokedamp in the aftermath of the explosion. It was described as a 'suffocating atmosphere'.

One man was found dead with a boy he had been carrying on his shoulders. Another was discovered still alive, struggling against the effects of chokedamp in a bid to find his missing sons, aged 16 and 22. A third miner descended the pit in an attempt to locate his son and was overcome by the chokedamp or perhaps carbon monoxide. He was brought to bank, dead. Historian M.A. Richardson declared the men had displayed a devotion to others and a courage 'that would have ennobled human nature in any rank of life'.

The inquest jury reached the conclusion that a miner had taken a candle into a working area where gas was present. It recommended that the use of candles should be discontinued and lamps introduced.

Today, a handsome building with tall windows and an

adjoining building to the rear, housing the shaft, with a pair of pithead wheels, survive at the site of the St Hilda Colliery. They date from c1900 and are situated in Henry Robson Way, off Station Road, South Shields, close to the entrance to the Tedco Business Works. Not far away, nearer the Market Place, is another wheel, erected as a memorial to those unfortunate 51 men and boys.

Collection of the Hatton Gallery, Newcastle University

A Thomas Hair watercolour of St Hilda Colliery, South Shields, c1840.

On September 28, 1844, another tragedy occurred in the Durham coalfield. A total of 95 men and boys died when an explosion engulfed the Little Pit at Haswell Colliery, a few miles west of Easington. Only four miners survived. These lucky men had been near the bottom of the shaft at the time of the blast. A line of full tubs in a rolleyway shielded them from the full effects of the conflagration, although their pony was lost. The rest of the men and boys in the pit were killed by the explosion or by afterdamp.

The four survivors raised the alarm. Would-be rescuers attempted to enter the Meadows and Brockley Whins Flats areas but were initially driven back by the foul air. When they eventually entered these areas they found the dead. Some had perished from burns, but most had succumbed to the effects of afterdamp. One man was discovered with his cap in his mouth. He had been attempting to stop himself inhaling the

International Maritime

St Hilda Colliery in the 1890s, from a similar vantage point.

North of England Institute of Mining and Mechanical Engineers Bell-5-53

To all concerned in Coal Mines.

MR JUSTICE BAYLEY,

In his Address to the Grand Jury, at the Durham Spring Assizes, in 1824, alluded to the Explosion of a Coal Mine. He observed, "If those Persons who had the Care of such Concerns did not use proper Caution (whether that Want of Caution arose from the Use of improper Lamps, or from whatever other Cause), in the Event of Death ensuing they would be liable to the Charge of

MANSLAUGHTER."

W. A. Mitchell, Printer, Newcastle.

A newspaper records a judge's warning over coalmine explosions.

Whatever the cause, the bodies of the 95 men and boys were recovered and brought to bank. The village of Haswell went into mourning. Blinds were drawn and most shops closed. The *Sunderland and Durham County Herald* reported that few people in the village 'had not some relative or friend who was dear to them in the pit at the time'.

Today, a memorial to the Haswell victims stands next to the ruins of the pit's winding engine house. It is relief sculpture in the lower part of a large, white stone and depicts the faces of men, women and children in a coal seam or mine tunnel. The work, by sculptor Michael Disley, is entitled *The Spirit of Haswell*. Each of 95 railings fronting the memorial also carries a face, symbolising the victims. The inscription below the stone includes the words: 'Their spirit lives on.'

deadly fumes, in the same way as the lads at Wallsend in 1835. Other miners were found with their fingers over their mouths. Many of those who died were putters in their teens. Several boys were aged only 10, 11 and 12.

The exact cause of the Haswell explosion was never determined, but two Davy lamps were found damaged and it was thought the flame of one or both may have come into contact with methane released by a fall of stone from the roof or a fall of coal from a pillar. Another theory was that the fall had stirred up a current of air which caused the flame to pass through the gauze of a lamp. The pit was said at the time to be 'one of the best ventilated collieries in the mining district'.

Tom Yellowley

A detail view of The Spirit of Haswell, the memorial sculpture by Michael Disley, at the site of the old colliery engine house. The artwork commemorates the 95 men and boys lost at Haswell.

The Fatfield Colliery disaster

One of the earliest recorded pit disasters in the North East was the Fatfield tragedy of August 18, 1708. An explosion at the Fatfield pit, not far from the River Wear, killed 69 people. Today a plaque, somewhat difficult to spot, is sited near the location of the old mine at the junction of Biddick Lane and Fallowfield. It lies beneath a white willow, planted in 1987 as a memorial to those who lost their lives. The dead included at least one woman. A further explosion at the same pit in 1767 killed 39. Two women were recorded among the casualties.

Another plaque, put up by Washington Development Corporation on a small building only a few yards away, tells visitors that sycamore, maple and beech trees were planted along Biddick Lane to replace an avenue of elms planted as a memorial soon after the disaster. The replacement trees are also a tribute to the hundreds of others who died in mining accidents throughout the Fatfield and Harraton district.

Other early disasters involving appalling loss of life included an explosion at the Bensham Colliery, Gateshead, in 1710. The accident is poorly recorded, but it may be that up to 80 lost their lives, possibly including women. The loss of female workers in such conflagrations may be the reason why from c1770-80 no women or girls were employed underground in North East mines.

A woman and two children move a tub of coals, enlarged from Matthias Dunn's technical manual of 1848, 'The Winning and Working of Collieries'. Women and girls were not employed in North East mines from the late 18th century.

The Fatal Beam

'Cage: A frame of iron which works between slides in a shaft.'

The centuries will burn rich loads
with which we groaned …
But they will not dream of us poor lads
lost in the ground.
        From 'Miners' by Wilfred Owen

A memorial in Earsdon Churchyard, North Tyneside, bears the names of the 204 men and boys killed in the New Hartley Pit disaster of 1862. The death toll was the highest of all the mining tragedies to hit the Great Northern Coalfield. Three of those who died at New Hartley were boys aged only 10, two were 11 and no less than 10 lads were aged 12. Fathers died along with their sons and brothers along with their brothers. One older miner perished with three of his sons and a grandson.

From parts of the churchyard the old Fenwick Pit spoil heap can be seen in the distance, a reminder that mining in this area was carried on well into the second half of the 20th century. The churchyard is, like most churchyards, a peaceful place. It is hard to imagine the day when thousands gathered at this spot to see the victims interred in graves, some communal, around where the monument now stands. The largest grave contained 33 of the dead.

The New Hartley Colliery had only one shaft leading to the Low Main Seam where the miners were working. It was to prove a fatal drawback and led Parliament to pass a law requiring every mine to have at least two shafts so that escape

Tom Yellowley

The memorial to the 204 men and boys killed in the New Hartley Colliery disaster of 1862. It was the Great Northern Coalfield's worst mining accident.

was still possible if one became blocked.

The disaster happened on the morning of January 16, 1862, when part of the pumping engine beam, which projected out over the mouth of the Hester Pit at New Hartley Colliery, broke off and crashed down the shaft. As it fell, this heavy, cast iron beam destroyed the wooden bratticing (partition) which divided the upcast and downcast airways and tore away the shaft's wooden lining. This resulted in a mass of tangled wreckage blocking the shaft, which was the only means of escape for the men and boys below.

The beam had broken away at the most unfortunate time possible. Most of the fore-shift or day men had only shortly before descended the pit and most of the back-shift or night men had not yet left the mine. Eight men were ascending in the cage when the beam plunged down. Five of them were killed, one of them slipping from the loop of a rope lowered in an attempt to rescue him. Three men were eventually hauled to safety. They were to be the only survivors.

A drift tunnel connected to a chimney-like way, known as a stapple, led upwards via a ladder from the Low Main Seam, where the men had been working, to the Yard Seam. The trapped miners took this route but on reaching the Yard Seam found their exit via the main shaft blocked by the mass of wreckage.

A tremendous effort was launched by pitmen from New Hartley, the surrounding districts and further afield to rescue the trapped men and boys by clearing the shaft of the wreckage. Miners were lowered, at great risk to themselves, on a chain for hourly shifts, with two men at a time extracting the debris and passing it upwards to others stationed at intervals on the sides of the shaft. Progress was painfully slow and six days went by. At first, the trapped

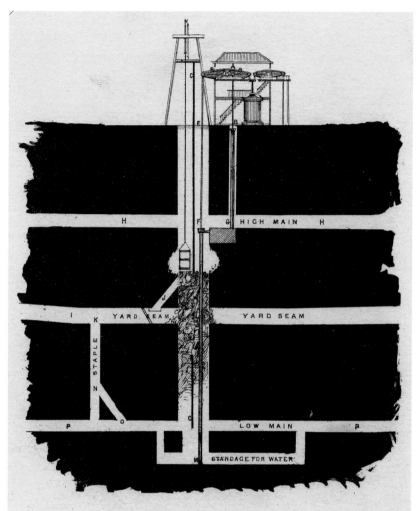

North of England Institute of Mining and Mechanical Engineers NRO 3410ZD-44-1/(82)

A diagram of the Hester shaft of New Hartley Colliery, showing the wreckage which blocked escape for the men and boys below.

miners were heard making a noise from the Yard Seam to encourage their would-be rescuers. Eventually the noises ceased.

Author T. Wemyss Reid penned a day-by-day account of

A scene at the New Hartley pithead shortly after the disaster, from the Illustrated London News, 1862.

the efforts to reach the men: 'Volunteers from all parts of the district, responsive to the call for help, have hastened to the scene of the catastrophe. All this morning, little bands were seen approaching the place from north, south and west, and as they arrived they simply and modestly announced that they had "come to help".' The weather at this time was bitterly cold, with winds blowing in from the North Sea.

Things did not go well. The rescue work was delayed when part of the stone wall lining the shaft fell away and added to the mass of tangled wreckage. After nearly a week of work three men managed to reach the Yard Seam, where the bodies of 199 miners were found. It seems they had succumbed to carbon monoxide gas. Another likely factor was a lack of oxygen and high level of carbon dioxide. Both conditions would have been engendered by the ventilation furnace in the mine continuing to burn and smoulder. Added to the five killed in the shaft, the total death toll was 204.

Wemyss Reid reported that the man who led the first team into the seam had more than once seen 'the father clasping in his arms the son'. He had seen 'again and again, a group of children clustered around their father'.

A notebook was found in the pocket of the back-shift

North of England Institute of Mining and Mechanical Engineers NRO 3410ZD-44-1|07|

Men involved in the rescue attempt at New Hartley.

overman, James Amour, in which he recorded that a number of men had taken 'extremely ill'. They had held a prayer meeting while awaiting rescue. The overman's son, Richard, died along with his father.

The Methodist chapel in New Hartley was used as a makeshift morgue for the bodies to be identified. All the blinds were drawn in the village. Families who were Primitive Methodists held their own short funeral services in their homes before the main funeral.

Most of the coffins were carried on carts from New Hartley to Earsdon Church, a distance of nearly four miles. It was said that as the last cart left the village the first 'rough hearse' had arrived at the church. Thousands turned out to mourn the 204 men and boys. The Duke of Northumberland gave land next to the churchyard for burial of the bodies. Most were interred in three rows on this land and a few in the main churchyard. The tragedy shocked the nation.

Two years earlier, disaster had hit Burradon Colliery, not far from New Hartley. Two explosions on March 2, 1860, and the effects of afterdamp resulted in the deaths of 76 men and boys. The miners had complained of gas blowers and poor ventilation. Naked lights were still being used in many areas. But Burradon was by no means the only pit with low safety standards at this period. A memorial to the disaster victims, and to all those who died during the lifetime of the colliery, can be found on a small green by the main road through Burradon village. Incorporating a pit wheel, it is fronted by flower beds and a tub.

The human cost of all these accidents cannot be underestimated. For example, reporting on an explosion which claimed 22 lives at Hebburn Colliery on May 6, 1852, the *Newcastle Journal* stated: 'One of those who perished married a widow three months ago, with three children. She had been four times married and had lost three husbands by explosions.' A trapper boy was also among the victims.

The year 1880 witnessed a conflagration of terrible magnitude at Seaham Colliery in County Durham. This pit, owned by the Londonderry family, was always known as 'The Nack' or 'Nicky Nack' and had been the scene of several earlier explosions, including one on October 25, 1871, in which 26 men and boys died. Worse was to come.

On September 8, 1880, an explosion at this mine resulted in the deaths of 164 men and boys. The blast may have been caused by shot-firing or a safety lamp problem. The exact cause remains unknown. The pit was utterly devastated, with numerous roof falls.

Seaham Colliery was worked on three levels – there were 231 miners underground at the time – but the men who died all worked in the middle level. There were only four survivors from this area.

The memorial to all miners who lost their lives at Burradon Colliery.

Gas had not been reported before the explosion nor had any problems with ventilation been noted. Shot-firing by stonemen was considered the most likely cause, but there was no definite proof. Another theory was that one man's Clanny lamp in combination with over-rapid ventilation may have been to blame. Whatever the reason, coal dust was a potent factor.

Some men and boys were trapped in the Hutton and Maudlin seams after the blast and lived for a number of hours. A sad and poignant message, inscribed on a water container, was left by one man before he passed away: 'Dear Margaret, there were 40 of us altogether at 7am. Some were singing hymns but my thoughts was on my little Michael that him and I would meet in heaven at the same time. Oh dear wife, God save you and the children and pray for me. Dear wife, farewell. My last thoughts are about you and the children. Be sure and learn the children to pray for me. Oh what an awful position we are in.'

This unfortunate man's son, 'little Michael', is reported to have died on the same day as the disaster or the day before.

The memorial to the 164 victims is in the Garden of Remembrance at Christ Church, Seaham, opposite the site of the colliery, which closed in 1988. The names of the men and boys are inscribed in gold-coloured lettering on the face of the memorial, which is surmounted by a cross. An inscription reads: 'What man is he that liveth and shall not see death.' Only a few yards away, and also within the garden, is a memorial commemorating the 26 who died in the 1871 tragedy. Both tributes are within sight of the sea.

Scarcely less appalling than the 1880 Seaham accident was the explosion which resulted in the deaths of 74 miners at Trimdon Grange Colliery in the south of County Durham on February 16, 1882. Eight of the boys who died were aged only 13. It was found that a fall in the roof of a waste area had released methane with such force that the gas had blown through the gauze of a Davy lamp, igniting the blast. The pit was known to be particularly dusty. The Trimdon Grange workings were linked by a tunnel to the Kelloe Colliery and afterdamp from the explosion spread to this mine, killing six men there.

A memorial to the Trimdon Grange victims stands in the cemetery on the eastern edge of Trimdon Village. Forty-four

of the 74 are buried here. The stone memorial is surmounted by a cross and features relief carvings of a miner being rescued from a pit, a grieving widow and daughter at a graveside, a pitman with a lamp making his way to work and clasped hands symbolising friendship. The names of victims

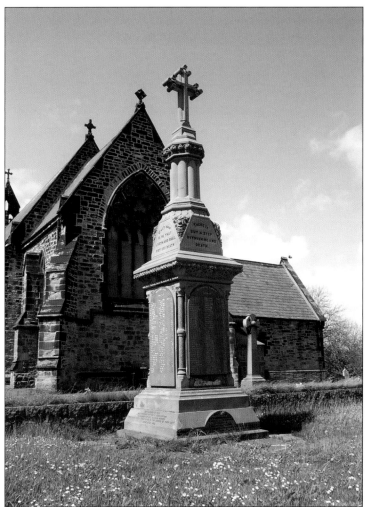

Richard Smith

The memorial at Christ Church, Seaham, to the 164 men and boys who died in the Seaham Colliery disaster of 1880.

Tom Yellowley

A miner is being rescued from a pit in this relief carving on the memorial to the Trimdon Grange disaster victims at Kelloe cemetery.

Tom Yellowley

A grieving mother and daughter are shown on the Trimdon Grange disaster memorial at Trimdon Village cemetery. The memorials are virtually identical.

appear on the face of the memorial and on stones surrounding it. Twenty-six more of the dead are buried at Kelloe Cemetery where a virtually identical memorial can be found. The inscription records that as well as the 26 at Kelloe, one victim is interred at Croxdale, one at Cassop cum Quarrington and two at Shadforth.

A blue-painted pithead wheel from the colliery is sited in Trimdon Grange as another memorial to the dead and also to Peter Lee, the miners' leader and Durham County Council chairman, who was born at Trimdon Grange in July 1864. The wheel is on the edge of a recreation ground off the main street.

Only two months after the Trimdon Grange conflagration, a similar tragedy hit Tudhoe Colliery. Firedamp set off an explosion on April 18, 1882, and 37

miners were lost A memorial to the dead was erected in Tudhoe cemetery, and is almost identical to the Trimdon Village and Kelloe ones. Three years later, on March 2, 1885, Usworth Colliery, north of Washington Village, was the scene of blast which killed 42 men and boys.

Britain had become the 'Workshop of the World' during the 19th century, building her industry and great empire on the backs of the pitmen. They played a fundamental role in Britain's economic expansion, but many lost their lives in a never-ending battle against subterranean perils, the greatest of which was firedamp.

Neville Hall, Newcastle

The North of England Institute of Mining and Mechanical Engineers was established in 1852 to promote safety in the pits and to set up a library on mining and mechanical engineering. Based at Neville Hall, close to Newcastle's Central Station and the monument to locomotive pioneer George Stephenson, the Institute today plays an important role in preserving the heritage of the collieries in the North East and provides a vital source of information on many aspects of mining, engineering and geology worldwide. The Institute was incorporated by Royal Charter in 1876.

Neville Hall, a superb example of a Gothic Revival building, was completed in 1872 to the designs of architect A.M. Dunn. It is a Grade 2* listed building. It contains the Nicholas Wood Memorial Library, which has a fine collection of papers, maps, journals and books relating to the subject. Nicholas Wood was the leading viewer of his time and the first president of the Institute. He was a close colleague of George Stephenson at Killingworth Colliery.

The library, which is open to the public (volunteers are also welcome), is housed in a magnificent hall featuring a lofty, arched ceiling with skylights, spiral staircases, and large stained glass windows at each end. Neville Hall also contains a fine lecture theatre. More details can be found on the Institute's website www.mininginstitute.org.uk.

Tom Yellowley

The Nicholas Wood Memorial Library at Neville Hall, Newcastle, home of the North of England Institute of Mining and Mechanical Engineers. Pictured is the fine stained glass window at the eastern end of the library. Another large window of stained glass adorns the western end.

Miners Advance

'What wrong are the workmen doing? Our only aim is the establishment of common justice amongst mankind.'
William Crawford, Durham miners' leader, defending trade unions against criticism

Coal coming out of a mine was inspected on the surface by an official known as a keeker. If the official found small coals, stones, or shale in a corf or tub the pitman responsible could be fined, thus reducing his wages. Corves or tubs suspected of containing too much unwanted material might be separated from the others and tipped out for inspection. This was known as 'laying out'. In addition to fines, a corve or tub deemed to be unsatisfactory might be forfeited to the company, so that the man would receive no money at all for the coal he had won.

Another rule concerning output was that each corve or tub had to contain the quantity of coal demanded, even though no debris was present. If a pitman failed to achieve this quantity his tub might also be laid out and forfeited to the company. These rules were open to abuse by employers and could mean that a man's pay might be greatly reduced.

It was only from the 1840s onwards that weight began to be widely adopted as a measure of the amount of coal. Prior to this, volume measurement was frequently used. North East industrial archaeologist Dr Stafford Linsley writes: 'The wage payment systems varied in time, and sometimes in place. However, the most common method of payment for hewers was based upon the amount of coal won, but not necessarily by weight, for volumetric measures were standard right up until the early 19th century. Typically, before the 1840s, the corves (large baskets of a specified size) filled by the miners would have to be 'wood full' of coal (ie level with the top of the basket – hence volumetric rather than weight measure) in order for them to be paid, and miners would also be penalised if any rubbish was mixed with the coal.'

Dr Linsley quotes a typical Bond document of 1770 which includes the words: 'The hewer of any corf not wood full when sent to bank shall forfeit the corf and the hewer that keeps not his coal clean from stones or any other refuse shall forfeit sixpence … Each corf to be and consist of eighteen pecks usual coal measure.'

Peter Burt, father of Northumberland miners' leader Thomas Burt, was said on one occasion to have had seven of his eight tubs of coal laid out. Thomas's uncle, Robert, had gone on strike at Seaton Delaval Colliery in a protest against excessive laying out, which could mean a man earned little or nothing for a day's hard work. Robert Burt had voted against the strike, cautioning moderation, but had nevertheless abided by the majority decision. Despite this, he was arrested for ceasing work without giving notice and sentenced, with others, to two months hard labour.

The unfair or over-zealous application of these controversial regulations was deeply resented by the miners who were nearly always working in a dim light. Bands of coal interspersed with stone were particularly difficult to separate in the darkness of a mine. These rules also offered scope for victimisation of men who were considered active trade unionists or disliked for any reason.

Such conditions naturally caused a great deal of ill feeling

The Crane for Loading the Rollies, by Thomas Hair. Here a corve is being loaded on to a rolley for its journey to the shaft.

and upset. But the spark which re-ignited trade unionism in the Great Northern Coalfield was the move by the owners to re-introduce the yearly Bond from 1864. This provoked an outcry among the men. The employers also demanded a wage reduction.

A meeting of largely Northumberland miners was held on Christmas Day 1863 at Horton, near Blyth, to discuss the situation. It was reported that around 4,000 pitmen attended. Inspired by memories of Hepburn's Union and led mainly by Primitive Methodists, they agreed to resist the imposition of a yearly Bond and wage reductions. The men marched to the gathering led by a band. Banners from the strike of 1844, many of them by this time tattered, were unfurled after being hidden away in the cottages of men who still cherished the memory of Hepburn. Now they were again held high as trade unionism began to revive in the Great Northern Coalfield. This resistance to the yearly Bond seems to have proved successful in Northumberland with the employers dropping the idea.

Following the demonstration at Horton, a group of Northumberland miners, some of them veterans of the 1844 dispute, met in January 1864 on Newcastle Town Moor and founded a new union. A short time afterwards some of the larger collieries of County Durham joined their association.

However, this move towards a single association for both areas was reversed in the summer of 1864 when the Northumberland pitmen set up their own union and broke away from their brothers in Durham, founding the Northumberland Miners' Mutual Confident Association (which became known by the shorter title, the Northumberland Miners' Association). Evidently, the Durham miners were not averse to this split and also wished to form their own union.

For about a year William Crawford, a strong personality, was secretary of the Northumberland miners, but he left to take up another post. In 1865 Thomas Burt, a young Choppington pitman, was elected secretary of the Northumberland Miners' Association (NMA).

He took up the leadership during a strike for a wage increase at Cramlington Colliery. Once more, miners and

MEETING OF MINERS.

On Saturday, a monster meeting of miners, numbering several thousands, from various parts of Northumberland and Durham, was held on Newcastle Town Moor. About eleven o'clock bands of music, followed by hundreds of men, began to arrive on the Cowhill. A little before twelve o'clock the assembly had swollen to perhaps five or six thousand. Bands were playing, flags (all bearing mottoes relating to unity and co-operation) were fluttering, and men and youths were sauntering about; some of them, notwithstanding the cold, actually sitting upon the grass. The day was anything but suitable for an open air demonstration, the cold being most intense. Several hundreds went away before the meeting began; no doubt, in consequence of the severity of the weather. About 12 o'clock a waggon arrived upon the grounds. Several persons immediately got on, and business proceeded.

The Newcastle Courant for January 15 1864 reports the meeting of Saturday January 9 1864 on Newcastle Town Moor.

their families were evicted from their homes. A cross was marked on the door of each family facing eviction. Among those targeted was the treasurer of the union, Thomas Baulks, his wife and children who were put out into the street during heavy rainfall. A clash between miners and so-called 'candymen' – men hired to do the work of turning people and furniture out of the homes – resulted in the evictions being temporarily halted. Later, however, soldiers were drafted in, the evictions completed and arrests followed.

Several pitmen were sentenced to months of hard labour as a result. The strike ended in defeat for the miners after 20 weeks.

Despite this, the choice of Burt as secretary proved to be an excellent one. He urged the men to refrain from further disturbances or violence during the Cramlington dispute. A believer in arbitration, compromise and reasoned argument, he was a fervent campaigner for the union, an eloquent spokesman and an able negotiator. Burt visited many colliery villages, speaking at evening meetings and boosting membership. By 1873 the NMA had around 19,000 members.

Efforts at reviving large-scale trade unionism to the south of the Tyne did not prove successful at first, although trade union activity took place at individual pits. However, the Durham Miners' Association was formed in 1869 following a strike earlier that year at Monkwearmouth Colliery, Sunderland. The pitmen at this mine had withdrawn their labour in a bid to win better wages after a period of severe reductions. Four Monkwearmouth men were arrested and charged with breaking the Bond by leaving their work. They appeared before magistrates at Sunderland.

At the hearing, W.P. Roberts, a brilliant defence lawyer who became known as the 'Pitmen's Attorney General' or 'Pitmen's Attorney' for his dedicated work for the miners, argued that if a man was unable to read, then the mine owners should prove that the terms of the Bond had been read to him so that he fully realised the legal conditions under which he was bound.

Roberts revealed that one of the men could not read or write and the terms of the contract had not been read to him. He had signed the contract with his mark. The highly talented barrister contended that a man who was unable to read the Bond could not be held to abide by its terms. His arguments threw the prosecution into disarray. Roberts had exposed the legal weakness of the Bond system.

The owners now agreed to a proposal to cancel the Bond

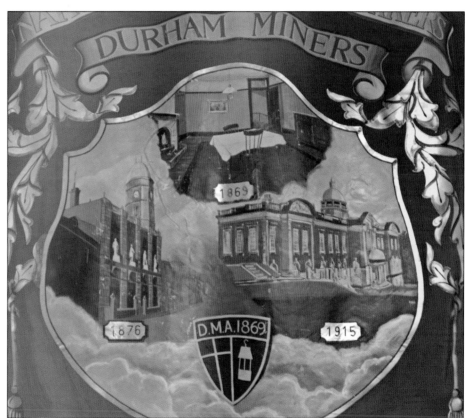

Tom Yellowley

An NUM banner depicts three key meeting places in the history of the Durham Miners' Association. Top, a room used for early meetings in the Market Tavern, Durham City. It was here that the DMA was founded in 1869. Left, the Miners' Hall in North Road, Durham City. Right, Red Hills, also in the city.

if the men left their colliery houses. This they did, and moved into makeshift accommodation. They also quit their jobs. The Bond was dropped. The case had sparked a revolt by a large number of the other men employed at Monkwearmouth, who had also decided to leave their houses and jobs rather than work under the 'villainous and iniquitous' Bond.

John Wilson (*A History of the Durham Miners' Association 1870-1904*) writes: 'The men formed in procession, over 300 in number, each man carrying his lamp and a copy of the colliery rules. Marching to the colliery they handed in their lamps and returned the rules to the overman.' The revolt now spilled over to the deputies who also threatened to quit their houses and employment. Faced with the threat of the colliery standing idle, the owners gave way and cancelled the Bond for all the workforce on condition the miners resumed work.

The solidarity shown by the pitmen of Monkwearmouth had defeated the Bond at their mine, and the outcome of the case gave a tremendous impetus to the revival of trade unionism in the county. After a few preliminary meetings, the Durham Miners' Association was founded by pitmen from various districts at a meeting at the Market Hotel, Durham City, in November 1869. The cancellation of the Bond at Monkwearmouth had been a catalyst.

The new union went on to achieve a considerable degree of success and by 1873 had 216 lodges and around 35,000 members, telling evidence of the large number of pits in County Durham. William Crawford became their secretary. Also by 1873, the Northumberland and Durham pitmen were members, through their unions, of the National Association of Miners.

In 1871 the Northumberland union, led by Burt, had met

The Miners' Hall, North Road, Durham City, which opened in 1876. The building still stands, but the Durham miners moved their headquarters to Red Hills in 1915. Note the statues of prominent leaders on the facade. These were also moved to Red Hills.

the employers, holding formal negotiations for the first time. This was to call for a 10-hour day for boys. Eventually, a compromise of 11 hours was agreed. The masters and men were at last talking.

However, the yearly Bond system still survived in County Durham despite the Monkwearmouth case and in January

1872 there was a large miners' demonstration at Easington against the continued use of this oppressive contract. The meeting was reported to have been attended by around 3,000 hewers from various collieries. They passed a resolution which stated: 'That we solicit our masters for a shorter period of agreement to abolish the yearly binding and substitute for it a fortnightly agreement.' The resolution was carried unanimously. Fortnightly contracts were already the norm in Northumberland.

In February 1872 the Durham union entered into negotiations with the Coal Trade Association, representing the mine owners, who had no doubt taken note of the strong groundswell of feeling among the men. Ten union delegates represented around 20,000 pit workers. The talks were held in Newcastle and the owners almost at once agreed to end the infamous yearly Bond system. The employers offered a 20% pay rise for underground workers. It was a wonderful double victory for the Durham miners at what was clearly a favourable time for the pits economically.

The talks were amicable. The union delegates 'thanked the masters most kindly for the manner in which they had met them' on the question of the Bond. It was reported that the owners had admitted the men 'ought to share the present prosperous position of the trade'. The representatives of the men agreed to make up the work time spent at the meeting to show their goodwill.

Among those present at this historic first meeting were William Crawford, the Durham Miners' Association leader, and Tommy Ramsey, a veteran of the 1844 strike and fervent advocate of trade unionism.

Further talks between the Durham union and mine owners were held in March and the pitmen accepted the 20% pay offer, although they still felt they were not receiving a fair share of the profits the owners were making. But men and masters were at last talking in Durham too. It was a great

Gateshead Libraries & Arts

Miners pose for a picture at Kibblesworth Colliery, near Gateshead, c1900.

advance on the previous years of fierce conflict and the employers' refusal to hold proper negotiations.

Fortnightly agreements instead of the annual Bond now became the norm in Durham to the delight of the men. A meeting was held at Thornley at which around 5,000 miners, their wives and children celebrated this momentous advance. Holding their banners proudly aloft, the pitmen and their bands marched through the neighbourhood. Speakers at the meeting stressed the advantages of unity. Support for the Durham Miners' Association grew. Afterwards, a 'soirée' was held at the Robin Hood Inn attended by miners, their wives and children at which 'everyone enjoyed themselves most heartily'.

A soirée and public meeting were also held at the Co-op Hall, Tantobie, near West Tanfield, again organised by the DMA. A 'substantial tea' was provided and afterwards Durham secretary William Crawford spoke about the abolition of the yearly Bond. It seems that relations with the Northumberland miners were good, for their leader, Thomas Burt, also attended. Displaying superb wit, Burt said he 'never liked to strike a man when he was down, and as the yearly Bond was killed outright, it would not be necessary to occupy the meeting with that subject'.

Meanwhile, also in July 1872, the Durham pitmen held further negotiations with their employers and achieved a wage rise of 15%. The owners had wished to exclude pony putters, but the union was unhappy with this and eventually the employers gave way.

However, in 1874 the Durham miners were forced to concede a 9% cut in wages following arbitration. By this time, miners both north and south of the Tyne had won the right to appoint their own checkweighmen. Checkweighmen were experienced and trusted miners chosen by the men to make sure that a face worker's output was weighed correctly at bank so that he did not suffer unjust reductions in pay. They frequently became union officials and acted as spokesmen for the miners.

An Act of Parliament coming into force in 1861 had stipulated that coal should be weighed – but failed to make payment of wages by weight compulsory. It allowed the pitmen to appoint at their own cost a man to witness the weighing of coals, but the mine owner was able to dismiss him or refuse to work with him. This legislation also banned any boy under 12 years of age from working underground unless he could produce a certificate that he could read or write. Pit lads were required to attend school for five hours per day.

Major improvements came with the Coal Mines Regulation Act of 1872. This allowed miners to choose their own checkweighman without the need for him to be approved by the management. It was now more difficult for the mine owner to dismiss him. The new law, coming into force in 1873, also stipulated that miners were to be paid by the weight of coals, instead of by measure. The Act restricted the hours of boys to a maximum of 10 bank to bank, and banned miners under the age of 18 from being put in charge of any machinery or apparatus on which the lives of men depended.

Other changes took place. Agreements were concluded between the miners and employers whereby wages were linked to 'sliding scales' for a set period. This meant the men's pay varied according to the changing price of coal. Sliding scales became the norm for many years in the North East. In Durham, the first such scale was introduced in March 1877 for a period of two years and it applied to hewers only. It was a formula for relative peace on the wages front, even if it meant that the miner and his family lived in constant uncertainty over their level of income as their wages were subject to fluctuation.

In 1879, a proposal by the employers for a wages reduction of 20% as a condition for renewing the sliding scale was met with opposition from the Durham union. The resulting strike lasted seven weeks, with the men accepting a cut, but this was greatly reduced from the one originally proposed following arbitration by Lord Derby, who was appropriately known as the 'Umpire'. In 1892, a major strike took place in the Durham coalfield against a reduction, but was unsuccessful.

Linking wages to the price of coal was a way of trying to avoid frequent disputes. However, the other wages link – to the amount of coal a man could produce – was particularly unfair since the small section of a mine worked by one man could differ greatly to the section worked by another. If a miner found himself in a low-roofed workplace, where in cramped, narrow and perhaps damp conditions the coal was difficult to win, his output would understandably be much

Northern Echo

Miners climb onto the roofs of their homes as action is taken to evict them during a strike at Silksworth Colliery in 1891. Furniture and other household items are being put into the street by bailiffs as police hold back the crowds. The following year, County Durham miners went on strike against a wage reduction.

lower than the man who had a more favourable spot. In addition, working in a poor light, small coals, stone and shale could easily be put into a tub without the miner realising. The answer to this problem was a guaranteed minimum wage, but the achievement of this was far in the future.

A practice had grown up in the North East pits known as

cavilling. This was the drawing of lots to determine the workplace – known as a cavil or stall – of each face worker. This was usually done quarterly on Cavilling Day. Stafford Linsley writes: 'Cavilling seems to have been common, if not universal, on the main coalfields of Northumberland and Durham, lasting at least until the 1960s, and having its origins in the mists of time. It seems to have been peculiar to the North East. The system meant that it was pot luck whether you worked in a difficult part of the pit or an easier part for any given quarter. It also meant that union men could not be so easily victimised by the managers/owners.'

In 1890 came one of the greatest victories for the Durham pitmen. Their union won for the hewers a seven-hour working day bank-to-bank. For putters the shift was cut from an average of 12 hours to 10.

Durham led the way in this respect. It was only in 1908 that legislation limited the working day for all miners throughout the country to no more than eight hours, and even this did not include the time spent descending, walking to the coalface, which could be several miles, and returning to bank. However, it was the first time the hours of men in the pits had been limited by law, rather than by agreement.

Also in 1908, the Durham union joined the Miners Federation of Great Britain (MFGB), which had been formed in 1889 and had agitated for the eight-hour day. The Northumberland miners had joined the federation in 1907. Before this the pitmen of Britain were split between the MFGB and the older National Association of Miners, which was strongly supported in the North East. The MFGB's campaign for an eight-hour day had made the Durham union wary of joining the federation, since their hewers already had a seven-hour day and it was feared the legal imposition of eight hours would upset shift arrangements and lead to a

longer working period for hewers. However, with the coming of the eight-hour day the Durham miners were able to secure the status quo of seven hours for hewers. The putters' hours were cut from 10 to eight.

The affiliation of the Northumberland and Durham unions to the MFGB was a momentous step. Pitmen throughout the country were now united into a single organisation with a total membership of nearly 600,000. The federation now had the strength for concerted action nationwide. In 1912, the MFGB staged a strike for a national minimum wage so that the livelihoods of miners would no longer be totally dependent on piecework and the price of coal.

In 1912 Britain too had a total dependency – on coal itself. Understandably, the government intervened in the dispute and the MFGB somewhat reluctantly agreed to a system which would allow minimum wage rates to be set at district level. The idea of a national minimum was thrown out by the government, much to the delight of the mine owners.

This settlement carried with it the implication that men in some areas would end up taking home less pay than their brother miners in other districts. This would have a tendency to divide miners. In addition, wage levels would be kept down because the men would lack the combined strength arising from national bargaining.

No miner, understandably, wanted to be reduced to the minimum wage. The piecework element of a pitman's wages remained despite the minimum rates, but piecework was also subject to the district system of determining rates.

The weighing of tubs continued well into the 20th century, after which payments were made according to the amounts extracted from the coalface, since conveyor belts

A miner putting a tub at Stargate Colliery, on the southern edge of Ryton, in the 1950s. Shorts and hoggers (stockings or socks) were usual wear at many pits. In low-roofed working areas hand putting continued well into the 20th Century.

rather than tubs were being used. The advent of highly mechanised longwall working in the 20th century brought another change. Where this modern system was used, with shearer machines and power loading, men were paid per shift, but with bonuses for the amounts extracted.

The National Union of Mineworkers was formed in 1945, its strength reflecting the strength of character and solidarity of the pitmen. The new union superseded the MFGB. The miners had advanced a long way since the days of the yearly Bond. Their indissoluble brotherhood had been forged amid danger, hardship and conditions of near slavery. It was a fraternity without equal.

The Rocking Strike

In 1863, the County Durham collieries owned by Straker and Love – Sunnybrow at Willington, and Brancepeth and Oakenshaw near Willington – were affected by a dispute over the tub system. At Sunnybrow, the pitmen found the tubs they filled to capacity underground were reaching bank with levels of coal deemed unsatisfactory by the keeker. Many tubs were confiscated because of this, the keeker being only too happy to have them laid out because he received a commission. The miners were losing eight to ten tubs each a fortnight. They complained that the tubs were not large enough to hold the amount they were expected to put into them.

Tom Yellowley

According to Fynes, the coal was packed as closely as possible, but in the low places in which men had to work the tubs were jolted as they went outbye, the coal being shaken down. To combat this effect, the men began the practice of 'rocking' the tubs so that the coal slipped down before being taken outbye and the tubs could be topped up. This rocking process was extremely hard and 'painful' work. Alternatively, the miner might strike the tub with his mel (long-handled heavy hammer) to shake the coal down before topping-up.

The pitmen went on strike over the issue, calling for wages to be paid according to the weight of coal in the tubs rather than on the basis of the number of 'full' tubs. They also sought a 5 per cent pay increase. Despite the new law of 1861 that tubs should be weighed, the degree to which they were filled was clearly still being used as an excuse to deprive men of money. Payment of wages by weight was not made compulsory by law until 10 years after the strike.

Mine owner Joseph Love did eventually agree to weight payment, but tubs not reaching the required weight were still to be laid out. He was determined to stamp out union activity at his collieries. So-called ringleaders of the strike were taken into police custody. At Sunnybrow, men on strike together with their wives and children were evicted from their colliery houses in cold weather. Constables and candymen were drafted in by the owners and furniture was dragged into the street or put on colliery carts, some of it being damaged by rough handling. Thirty-seven families were turned out to face the elements. Tents and camps were improvised in nearby fields. Later, the evicting party visited Oakenshaw and again men, women and children were turned out of their homes. They included pregnant women.

In 1976, a memorial to the men of the Rocking Strike was unveiled at Sunnybrow by NUM president Joe Gormley. Appropriately, it features a tub on rails atop a stone plinth. The memorial is located on the edge of the village on a green expanse of hillside overlooking the Wear Valley. As well as the strike, it also commemorates all the men and boys who lost their lives in the mines of Sunnybrow, Brancepeth and Oakenshaw.

Three Great Union Leaders

'There is always a kindly brotherliness about him.'
(a journalist writing about Thomas Burt)

Thomas Burt, the Northumberland miners' union leader, was born in 1837 in a row of cottages between Wallsend and North Shields, the son of a pitman. Thomas and his family moved to Whitley (now Whitley Bay) while he was still a small boy and his father, Peter, worked at a colliery there. Later, the family moved to Seghill Colliery. His father was a Primitive Methodist and an ardent trade unionist. During the 1844 strike the family were evicted from their tied cottage at Seghill. The young Thomas saw the family's furniture and belongings unceremoniously brought out of their cottage and dumped in the street by the 'candymen'. Other families were evicted at the same time. The evictions were overseen by constables armed with swords.

The family later moved to County Durham. At the age of 10 Thomas became a trapper boy at Haswell Colliery, and later worked as a donkey driver at the same pit. During this period he narrowly escaped being crushed to death by a descending pit cage. A miner saw the danger and pulled the lad to safety with only moments to spare. On another occasion, he was so exhausted he fell asleep while on trapper duty.

Thomas went on to work as a pitman at several other mines, including Sherburn, County Durham, and a long stint at Seaton Delaval Colliery, Northumberland. Other pits where he was employed included New Hartley, Choppington and Cramlington. Becoming an active trade unionist like his

Thomas Burt, leader of the Northumberland Miners' Association.

father, in 1865 Thomas was elected secretary of the Northumberland Miners' Association at the age of 27.

At the 1874 general election he stood as a Radical Labour candidate for Morpeth, with Liberal Party support. Thomas won and became one of the first two miners to be elected to Parliament. He served as MP for the constituency until 1918, a period of over 40 years. He was one of the first so-called Lib-Lab MPs. These were working or 'labouring' men who sat in the House of Commons with Liberal support. In 1892 Liberal Prime Minister William Gladstone appointed him Parliamentary Secretary to the Board of Trade and he served in this post for three years.

A journalist, writing in the 1890s, declared that the pitmen's leader was 'plain spoken only when he sees that a straight word of counsel may help his brother, but he is never censorious, and there is always a kindly brotherliness about him'. A friend of Thomas said: 'Tommy Burt is the best little fellow that ever stepped in shoe leather.' Of his chairmanship of the Trades Union Congress meeting in 1891 an observer wrote: 'It was a magnificent illustration of the sheer force of moral character. It was superb. The adroitness, the tact, the nimble-wittedness, and the good nature and self-possession which characterised him are beyond praise.'

Thomas Burt died in 1922 and is buried in Jesmond Cemetery, Newcastle. His name is commemorated in Burt Hall, Northumberland Road, Newcastle, almost opposite the City Hall. This building, opened in 1895, was the headquarters of Northumberland Branch of the National Union of Mineworkers for many years. It is now part of Northumbria University. The inner main entrance door is decorated with stained glass windows depicting two safety lamps, and on the upper floor a meeting hall contains a fine stained glass window featuring shields with images of picks, shovels, a lamp, tub and other mining emblems.

The facade of Burt Hall is surmounted by a fine statue of a miner with a pick over his shoulder. The work is based on one of the figures in the popular Ralph Hedley painting of two pitmen entitled *Going Home*.

William Crawford was born in Northumberland and worked at various pits in the county, including Cowpen. He was the leader of the Northumberland miners for about a year after the formation of the Northumberland

William Crawford, pioneer of the Durham Miners' Association.

Miners' Mutual Confident Association. Then he left to take up a job with the Co-operative Movement.

However, he did not stay long in this position, applying in 1870 for the post of agent with the newly-formed Durham Miners' Association. Crawford was known to the Durham miners from the days when pitmen from both sides of the Tyne were briefly united in a single union. Vying against a number of other candidates, he got the job and headed the Durham union during its formative years. Crawford spoke at the first Durham Gala in 1871 and the following year led the first delegation to meet the coal owners for official talks. It was at this meeting that the yearly Bond was abolished in County Durham.

John Wilson, the miners' MP, wrote of him: 'He had no superior and few equals in his grasp of and power to find a solution of, the peculiar difficulties and complications which arise in an occupation like the miners.' Wilson added that Crawford filled his post 'with a skill few men can command'.

William Crawford was elected Liberal-Labour MP for Mid-Durham in 1885 and like Thomas Burt remained loyal to the Liberals while espousing the cause of the working man and trade unionism as leader of the Durham miners. He died in 1890.

John Wilson, a close associate of Crawford, was one of the founders of the Durham union in 1869. He became its general secretary in 1896. Wilson also became a Liberal-Labour MP, being elected for Houghton-le-Spring in 1885. Defeated at an election the following year, he returned to the House of Commons as MP for Mid-Durham in 1890 following Crawford's death. John Wilson was made an honorary Doctor of Civil Law by Durham University in 1910 in recognition of his work as first president of the Durham Aged Minerworkers' Homes Association.

Perhaps the best-known Durham miners' leader was Peter Lee. Born at Fivehouses, Trimdon Grange, in 1864, Peter became a hewer while still a teenager and worked at several pits in the coalfield. Despite the long hours of work, he attended classes during his off-duty time and learned to read and write. Later, he travelled abroad, working briefly in America and South Africa, but on each occasion returned to his native County Durham. Peter went on to serve as checkweighman at Wingate and Wheatley Hill collieries. He then started a distinguished career in local government, becoming chairman of Wheatley Hill Parish Council. Later, he was elected to Easington Rural District Council.

Billy Middleton, of Thornley, is a member of the team that looks after the museum at the old chapel of rest in Wheatley Hill Cemetery, now the village heritage centre. The museum is partly devoted to the memory of this extraordinary miners' leader and councillor. The 1937 Wheatley Hill Lodge DMA banner, bearing Peter's portrait, takes pride of place at the centre of the exhibition. Also on display is a wooden lectern made by Peter, testimony to his days as a Primitive Methodist lay preacher.

'It was due to Peter Lee's efforts that the Wheatley Hill area got link roads, drains, a sewerage system, street lighting, an isolation hospital and its cemetery,' said Billy, a former blacksmith at the village colliery. 'Peter Lee had a very powerful personality.'

An imposing figure, Peter was tall, white-haired and white bearded. He lived at Wheatley Hill with his wife Alice for 19 years and his house still stands. 'He was an icon,' added Billy.

In 1909, Peter Lee was elected to Durham County Council and in 1919 became its chairman. It was the first Labour controlled council in the country. In the same year he was elected an agent of the Durham Miners' Association and served as its financial secretary. The former miner became DMA general secretary in 1930, holding this position until his death in 1935. He also played a leading role pressing for the creation of the Burnhope Reservoir in Upper Weardale to improve water supply in the county.

Fittingly, and at his own request, he was buried in the village cemetery he had fought so hard to provide. Alice lies at rest beside him. Their grave is close to the heritage centre. This exceptional man had a great affection for Wheatley Hill and its people. In turn, it seems the people still hold him close to their hearts. The nearby New Town of Peterlee is named after him – a fine tribute to a leader who worked hard for the miners and communities of County Durham.

A short distance away from Wheatley Hill is Thornley, where the Durham Mining Museum is based in the village community centre. Billy Middleton is proud of the pioneering role Thornley pitmen played in the foundation of the DMA. One of the first meetings which led to this development was held at Thornley, when men from 12 collieries were present. 'The meeting was held in a field at the top end of the village. They discussed the issues and had a picnic,' added Billy.

Richard Smith

The Wheatley Hill DMA Lodge banner celebrates miners' leader Peter Lee, who became chairman of Durham County Council. The New Town of Peterlee is named after him.

Tragedy at West Stanley

'From the humblest to the highest the expressions of sympathy were profound.'
Newcastle Weekly Chronicle, following the West Stanley disaster

Mining disasters in the Great Northern Coalfield continued to occur during the 20th Century. However, the focus on large-scale tragedies often belies the fact that accidents in which the death toll was in single figures were commonplace. Falls of stone or transport mishaps involving tubs would frequently kill a man or boy. Double figures of under 20 deaths also occurred with alarming frequency both in the 19th and 20th centuries. The larger-scale accidents occurred as peaks in a continuing catalogue of fatalities which amounted to thousands.

To this toll must be added the countless men who died from diseases engendered by dust, including pneumoconiosis and emphysema, as well as the suffering caused by long-term illness or injury.

One of the smaller peaks in this catalogue of tragedy was on October 14, 1906, when a firedamp blast led to the deaths of 26 miners at Wingate Grange Colliery in County Durham. Shot-firing was the cause. A memorial to the victims was erected in the main street of Wingate village. It takes the form of a fine sandstone obelisk bearing the names of the dead, with the poignant inscription 'Let them rest from their labours'.

However, barely three years after the Wingate tragedy a far greater disaster occurred at West Stanley Colliery, then often referred to as the Burns Pit. On February 16, 1909, the mine was hit by an explosion of great power. The West Stanley explosion killed 168 men and boys. Of these, 59 were

Tom Yellowley

A sandstone obelisk commemorates the 26 miners who died in the Wingate Grange disaster of 1906.

under the age of 20. A large number of those lost suffered terrible injuries, including burns, and many died from carbon monoxide poisoning or chokedamp in the wake of the explosion.

A group of survivors from the Tilley Seam gathered in an area which was free from the deadly fumes, to await rescue. A 14-year-old boy with broken legs was carried by some of the men. He lived for only a few hours. Eventually, a deputy named Mark

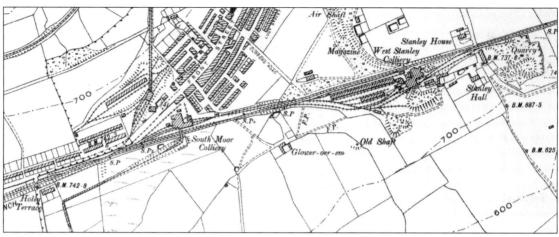

An Ordnance Survey map (1898) showing the site of West Stanley Colliery. 168 men and boys were killed in a disaster at this mine in 1909.

Henderson risked his life by leaving the group and braving the afterdamp to reach a telephone at the shaft bottom, about a quarter of a mile away. He told the officials at bank of the 26 survivors from the Tilley.

Both shafts of the Burns Pit were blocked with wreckage; the Busty Shaft was particularly badly affected. But the cages were intact and, after around 14 hours, the rescuers cleared the Busty Shaft and managed to reach the 26 survivors. Mark Henderson had gone back to his companions and guided them to the shaft in relays. Four men from the Towneley Seam (where the death toll was highest) were also rescued, although one died from the effects of the noxious fumes 30 hours after being brought to bank. An onsetter also survived.

Henry Davison, who had been working in the Tilley, said that the explosion 'kind of knocked me deaf'. He and other men had tried to reach the shaft more than once but were driven back by the foul air. They came across the boy with the broken legs, Jimmy Gardner, and carried him to the 'safe'

area. On their way, they found another boy and a deputy overman, both dead. A hewer named Carr looked after the injured Jimmy for three hours before he passed away.

Seventeen boys aged under 16 died in the tragedy. Three were aged only 13, four were 14 and ten 15. An extensive search failed to recover the bodies of two victims. The search was abandoned, but they were eventually found 24 years later – in 1933.

What had ignited this devastating coal dust explosion? An inquest jury was unable to provide the answer. Nor, after a thorough investigation, were the mines inspectors able to give a definite answer. The cause of the West Stanley tragedy remains a mystery. The death toll was the second highest of all the disasters to hit the Great Northern Coalfield.

On the day when most of the funerals were held, many thousands of people flocked to the streets of Stanley. The *Newcastle Weekly Chronicle* reported: 'The visitors in the village included men, women and children, old and young;

from the humblest to the highest the expressions of sympathy were profound.'

Today there are two main memorials to the West Stanley men and boys. One, of pink and grey marble in the cemetery at East Parade, Stanley, was erected in 1913 by social clubs of the district.

The most recent memorial, unveiled in 1995 by Newcastle United manager Kevin Keegan, grandson of one of the rescuers, is next to a green open space fronting the eastern end of the High Street in Stanley, close to Slaidburn Road. It features two impressive pit wheels and the names of the victims, together with the names of the seams they were working in on that fateful day. The memorial also bears an image of a West Stanley Lodge banner of the Durham Miners' Association. In front, a mosaic 'carpet' depicts a safety lamp, miner's shovel and pick. A plaque states: 'This memorial is also dedicated to all miners and their communities.'

The worst accident in the Great Northern Coalfield between the two world wars was at Montagu Colliery, Scotswood, Newcastle, on March 30, 1925. There were echoes of the Heaton Main tragedy when the Montagu View Pit was engulfed by an inrush of water from old mine workings. They turned out to be those of the former Paradise Pit, abandoned in 1848. This sudden flood led to the deaths of 38 men and boys.

The water burst through around half an hour after a deputy had fired two shots in the Brockwell Seam, the lowest part of the mine. The shots broke up a section of coal forming part of the 'wall' between the old and new workings. This 'wall' was now too thin to withstand the pressure of water. The deputy and hewers had, of course, been unaware that old workings were so perilously close.

Richard Smith

The impressive memorial to the 168 miners who died in the West Stanley Colliery disaster of 1909.

A trickle was reported by one of the hewers about 15 minutes after the shot-firing. A boy was sent to alert the deputy, Joseph Robson, who returned and decided to ask his young son, also working in the mine, to fetch an overman. Moments later the water burst through with great force. The deputy heard the noise, turned back towards the face and saw the flood rushing towards him.

Joseph's son, a putter and two pony drivers escaped, as well as a group of other miners who waded their way out. The deputy also escaped, but not before he had turned inbye to another area where men were working and led them to safety. An overman, Sam Evans, was lost when he went inbye in an attempt to rescue others but was cut off by the rising water. Another man, deputy William Johnson, was also lost as he tried to save his marras.

Many of the 38 victims at the Montagu View Pit were drowned and others, trapped by the flooding, succumbed to chokedamp. The accident might have been avoided had the deputies and overmen had access to plans of the old workings.

Author A.J. Cronin included scenes based on the Montagu disaster in his novel *The Stars Look Down*. A memorial to the victims in Elswick Cemetery features statues of a miner in shorts with safety lamp and pick, and of the Good Shepherd. In 2006, a memorial garden, with a pavement area on the theme of a pithead wheel, was created at St Margaret's Church, Scotswood.

On June 26 1942, during the Second World War, 13 miners died as the result of a blast at Murton Colliery.

On August 22, 1947, a blast led to 22 deaths at the Louisa Pit, Stanley. Not for the first time, firedamp combined with coal dust had proved lethal. It was believed that someone had struck a match to light a cigarette. Smoking is, of course, banned underground.

May 29, 1951 saw the deaths of 81 pitmen as the result of

The Montagu View Pit, Scotswood, Newcastle, where 38 men and boys died in 1925.

Tom Yellowley

Left, the statue of a pitman, complete with pick and lamp, on the memorial to the Montagu View Pit disaster victims. Right, crowds gather in the rain at the pithead on May 24, 1925, before the funeral of those who died at Montagu View.

a major firedamp explosion at Easington Colliery. The blast, in the so-called Duckbill District, was spread by coal dust for a distance of 16,000 yards. Two rescue workers also lost their lives in the resulting afterdamp.

The chief mines inspector found that the explosion had been started by a cutter machine coming into contact with pyrites. As the machine cut through the pyrites it produced a fine dust. The resulting friction caused the pyrites dust to overheat and spark. The sparks ignited firedamp which had accumulated in large cavities in the roof of the waste area behind a longwall face.

The alarm was soon raised but an attempt to telephone

the miners in the Duckbill District drew only silence. On the surface things were far from silent. Ambulance bells alerted Easington people and they gathered at the colliery gates. Sam Watson, general secretary of Durham Area NUM, and the Bishop of Durham, Dr Alwyn Williams, also went to the pithead.

Mine rescue teams from Houghton-le-Spring, Crook and Elswick in Newcastle tried to reach the affected district. It was a very difficult task. Heavy falls and thick afterdamp hampered their efforts. Two rescue workers, John Wallace and Harry Burdess, died from the effects of carbon monoxide, even though they were wearing breathing apparatus. Both were later found to have been suffering from forms of emphysema and this was a probable factor in their deaths.

One miner, Matthew Williams, aged 19, was brought out of the pit alive, but died soon afterwards from his injuries. Matthew's twin brother, George, had been working in another part of the pit at the time and his first reaction after the explosion was to search for a stretcher. He wanted to find his brother. However, George was ordered to return to bank because of the threat from afterdamp. Indeed, the first that George and his marras knew of the blast was when 'a great cloud of black gas came along the engine plane towards us'. The Easington death toll of 83 was the coalfield's highest since the Second World War.

There is a memorial to the victims in Easington Colliery Cemetery. Seventy two of the dead are buried side by side in a memorial garden at the centre of the cemetery, reached through an avenue of whitebeam trees. At one end of the garden is a relief sculpture of a miner, complete with helmet and carrying a safety lamp. Next to him is a large lump of coal surmounted by a cross. Flanking the relief are two coal-

A cutter machine is part of the Easington Colliery disaster memorial in the village cemetery.

filled tubs on rails. The inscription reads: 'Remember before God those who gave their lives in the Easington Colliery disaster in May Nineteen Hundred and Fifty One to whom this garden of remembrance is dedicated.' Close to the relief is a coal-cutting machine on rails. At the other end of the garden a relief facing the graves depicts safety lamps.

Across the main road through the village, an avenue of trees leading to Easington Colliery's Welfare Park also commemorates the dead. Each tree represents one of the victims. The first tree was planted by a 16-year-old miner in 1952. In the avenue a large stone from the scene of the disaster bears a memorial tablet urging passers-by to 'get understanding and promote goodwill in all things'.

Just a few weeks later, on July 6, 1951, nine miners lost their lives when firedamp exploded at Eppleton Colliery. The gas had come into contact with the electrics of a control box on a loader machine. An open gap was found in the covering of this box. Six of the nine victims died from carbon monoxide poisoning. Two others passed away from their injuries after the blast. A mines inspector concluded that coal dust played little, if any, part in the explosion. Firedamp was almost certainly the sole cause.

The mining community was still in shock when, on October 1, five men were killed in a blast at Weetslade Colliery, near Wideopen. Operations to recover the bodies of four victims took nearly two months, with rescue teams hampered by water and the danger of further explosions. The bodies were not discovered until late November. The cause of the explosion took a great deal of unravelling, but it was concluded that gas had probably interacted with the battery of a shuttle car.

The Weetslade tragedy brought the death toll from the disasters that year to 97, two more than in the Haswell tragedy over a century previously. It was a heart-rending illustration of the continuing dangers faced by pitmen.

In remembrance. A relief sculpture of a miner and a lump of coal surmounted by a cross on the Easington Colliery disaster memorial. The death toll was 83.

An artwork consisting of three stone and metal columns crowns the summit of the landscaped spoil heap of Weetslade Colliery, close to Wideopen and immediately north of Newcastle. The columns commemorate the mine and celebrate the site's new status as a country park. There is a fine view in all directions from the top of the heap, now transformed into a pleasant hill.

Help with Recovery

Conishead Priory at Ulverston, Cumbria, was a convalescent home and rehabilitation centre for injured County Durham miners from 1930 to 1971. It was also used by miners suffering from illnesses. The recovering pitmen were able to play bowls and putting in the beautiful grounds and take trips to the Lake District. The priory, on the shores of Morcambe Bay, must have seemed a world away from the industrial setting of the North East mines. Some injured Durham men also went to a rehabilitation centre known as The Hermitage at Chester-le-Street, opened during the Second World War, where games and other exercises were part of the therapy.

The Northumberland miners' rehabilitation centre and convalescent home was at Hartford Hall, near Cramlington. Here the pitmen were given therapy and exercises similar to those at The Hermitage. Former Algernon miner Jim Lucas is full of praise for the work carried out there by physiotherapists, nurses and doctors. Hartford Hall featured a model coal face where the miners were helped to deal with cramped spaces again. They also practised handling rocks.

Jim, who had suffered a spinal injury, was given warm brine baths to aid recovery. By the end of his stay, he and his fellow patients were carrying out various tasks in the hall's grounds. 'We went to the rehabilitation centre a raggle taggle group of men in plaster, we came out fit. If it hadn't been for Hartford Hall I would have been a cripple for life,' comments Jim.

In 1961, the Sam Watson Rest Home, at Richmond, North Yorkshire, was opened to provide holiday breaks for wives and widows of miners. It is still open today, and now caters for wives and widows from Northumberland as well as Durham. The home was named after Sam Watson, general secretary of Durham Area NUM for many years until his retirement in 1963.

Conishead Priory Convalescent Home is depicted on the Deaf Hill DMA Lodge banner.

The Great Lockout 1926

'Not a penny off the pay, not a second on the day'
A.J. Cook, general secretary, Miners' Federation of Great Britain

In 1917 the government took over control of the mines because of their vital importance to Britain during the First World War. National wage negotiations replaced the old district structure and these were successful in winning advances. The pitmen had come to realise that national determination of pay levels was the best way to improve their standard of living. This central negotiating structure went hand-in-hand with state control. Private coal owners were opposed in peacetime to such arrangements, and insisted on preserving the old district bargaining structure.

The miners knew from personal experience that under private ownership Britain's coal industry suffered from waste, inefficiency and a lack of investment in technical improvements such as coal cutting machines and conveyors. These problems, they contended, together with the need for improved safety, could best be tackled under common ownership. There were around 2,000 colliery owners in Britain and many – though not all – had a poor reputation as employers. Most seemed to resist change instinctively and were viewed by the miners as exploitative and reluctant to invest in improvements. The experience of wartime state control had reinforced the socialist belief that the mines should be run for the benefit of the whole people and not just for the profit of a privileged few.

In early 1919, while the pits were still under temporary government control, the Miners Federation of Great Britain called for public ownership of mines and minerals, a 30% wage increase and a six-hour working day. In addition, the federation proposed that the miners should share control of the collieries with management. The response of the coalition government, led by Lloyd George, to the strike threat was to propose that an inquiry be set up to look into the miners' claims and to examine the state of the coal industry. The government offered an extra shilling a day on wages to cater for an increase in the cost of living. The men rejected these proposals in a ballot.

Lloyd George then intervened and urged the MFGB leaders to postpone the strike and take part in the proposed commission of inquiry. At a conference held shortly afterwards, the MFGB decided to agree to the prime minister's plan, with the proviso that half the commission members should be appointed by the miners. The strike starting date was postponed.

After further talks, it was agreed that four members of the 13-strong commission would be chosen by the miners, that there would be three other workers' representatives chosen with the agreement of the miners and the government, plus three employers' representatives and three government representatives. The commission was to be chaired by a judge, Sir John Sankey.

Three differing interim reports were produced after the first stage of the inquiry. The six workers' representatives recommended that the 30% wage increase be granted along with a six-hour day for underground workers exclusive of winding times. The three employers' representatives recommended a pay increase of 1s.6d a day and a seven-hour day for underground workers. Judge Sankey and the three government nominees recommended a seven-hour day for underground workers from July 1919, which would be reduced to six hours from July 1921 if economic conditions were favourable, and a two shillings a day increase in wages.

The second stage of the inquiry examined the issue of public ownership. Among those giving evidence to the commission in favour of nationalisation was William Straker, general secretary of the Northumberland miners, who had succeeded Thomas Burt in 1913.

Unsurprisingly, the workers' representatives on the commission came down in favour of nationalisation and the employers in favour of continued private ownership. Two of the government representatives also rejected nationalisation and backed private ownership, with the third rejecting outright nationalisation but proposing amalgamation of collieries to form district 'trust' companies with a strong voice for the miners in their control. With six for and six against nationalisation, Judge Sankey was left with what might be described as the casting vote. He came down in favour of public ownership. Despite this, after several months of delay, Lloyd George's government rejected public ownership. The miners felt betrayed on this issue, but the working shift was reduced to seven hours.

Gateshead Libraries & Arts

Young putters and drivers from the last shift to reach bank at Addison Colliery, close to Ryton, before the 1926 lockout began. The pit village of Addison has now disappeared.

By the second half of 1920 the coal industry began to feel the effects of recession following the short post-war boom. The cost of living rose. Exports of coal slumped amid increased competition from foreign mines. In 1921 the government, alarmed at the losses suffered by the industry, handed back the mines to the control of the private owners. Faced with the recession, the owners demanded large wage reductions. The miners understandably rejected these terms and on the day the mines were transferred back to private ownership, March 31, 1921, a lockout began.

The miners had, in 1914-15, forged the Triple Alliance with the National Union of Railwaymen and the Transport Workers' Federation. They agreed to support one another with sympathetic strike action if in crisis. In 1921 the MFGB turned to its two allies for support. The rail and transport unions agreed to back the pitmen with a strike beginning on Saturday, April 16, aimed at halting the movement of coal.

An attempt by the government to resume negotiations was rebuffed by the miners, who felt there was nothing of any use to them on the table. The rail union was unhappy with this and their leader, J.H. Thomas, urged the MFGB to hold the talks. Then, without warning, the rail and transport unions called off their strike the day before it was due to begin. The miners felt they had been betrayed by their allies on what became known as 'Black Friday' (April 15, 1921). They were left to hold out, alone, against the coal owners and government, until, in July, they were forced to concede steep wage cuts.

In 1923-24 exports of coal revived for a short while. A strike in America and the French occupation of Germany's Rhur coalfield led to a temporary decline in foreign competition so the owners conceded wage increases. But in 1925 Britain returned to the gold standard and by this time foreign competition had revived. Exports were badly hit. The owners once more demanded major wage cuts and a longer working shift of eight hours. A crisis was inevitable.

The miners utterly rejected this double blow of low pay and longer hours. They accordingly asked the General Council of the Trades Union Congress for support in their battle to resist these demands. The General Council backed the pitmen and asked the rail and transport unions to stop the movement of all coal. However, the government interceded before the action could take place. Prime Minister Stanley Baldwin proposed that, as a temporary measure, the government would provide a subsidy to avert the pay cuts and longer hours. Meanwhile, another commission would look into the problems of the coal industry and propose a strategy for its future. The miners agreed on July 31, 1925. The date was dubbed 'Red Friday'.

Yet the looming crisis had only been postponed by Baldwin's intervention. The resulting Samuel Commission did not produce a report which pleased the miners. It recommended reorganisation of the industry and wage reductions as the only way forward. The MFGB, under the passionate leadership of its general secretary A.J. Cook, rejected the report. Both sides now prepared for battle. The subsidy ended on May 1, 1926, and the Great Lockout of the miners began. Heading the pitmen's determined resistance, A.J. Cook famously declared: 'Not a penny off the pay, not a second on the day.'

The TUC General Council called on large sections of Britain's workforce to strike in support of the miners and they responded with an astonishing display of solidarity. Thus it was that the Great Lockout triggered the General Strike, which began on May 4, 1926. Transport, gas, electricity, printing, iron and steel, and chemical workers were among those who took part in the stoppage. Newspapers were halted. The government issued its own newspaper, *The British Gazette*, edited by Winston Churchill. This publication tried to depict the strike as a threat to the constitution and a bid to bring about revolution. The leaders of the TUC had no such intent. The TUC accordingly brought out its own newspaper, *The British Worker*, to put the unions' case.

Mr. A. J. COOK, secretary of the Miners' Federation.

A.J. Cook.

Councils of Action were formed by miners in a considerable number of the Great Northern Coalfield's districts. Leading the way, and acquiring a reputation for militancy, were pitmen in the Chopwell district of County Durham, where Lenin Terrace, Marx Terrace and Owen Terrace can still be found.

The Blaydon and Chopwell Council of Action organised picketing of vehicles and even issued permits to lorries and vans carrying food. They published a strike newsletter entitled *The Northern Light*. One of the key figures behind this initiative was the chairman of Blaydon Urban District Council, Harry Bolton. As well as being a leading councillor, Harry was secretary of the DMA's Chopwell Lodge and a Justice of the Peace, being chairman of the Blaydon Bench of magistrates.

Harry and a leading official of the Durham union, Will Lawther, were arrested as they attempted to stop a food lorry which did not have a Council of Action permit and served a short spell in Durham Jail. Other picketing miners also served short prison terms in connection with attempts to restrict or obstruct transport.

Will Lawther was to become president of the MFGB and was elected a Labour MP in 1929. He eventually received a knighthood – under the Labour Government which took office in 1945 – for the help he gave miners during the Second World War. In 1945, he became the first president of the newly-formed NUM. Some people in the Chopwell area were unhappy with his acceptance of the knighthood.

MR. WILL LAWTHER. MR. HARRY BOLTON.

Newcastle Daily Chronicle, May 10, 1926.

The militancy of the Chopwell miners earned the village the nickname 'Little Moscow' – the lodge banner features portraits of Marx and Lenin as well as Keir Hardie. Jack Fletcher, a teacher who comes from a mining family and still lives in Chopwell, is the grandson of Harry Bolton. He stresses that the reputation of Chopwell for communism was unfair, although the miners were militant and there were a number of communists.

'My grandfather was a leading light in getting the portraits put on the banner and in the naming of the streets after Marx and Lenin,' he says. 'But he was not a communist. He was a Methodist and left wing socialist who believed in democracy. In the 1920s many socialists were unaware of the ruthless nature of the Bolshevik regime in Russia and saw the Revolution as the dawn of a Utopia. The reputation of Chopwell for communism was largely unfounded.'

Jack points out that Christianity, and in particular Methodism, had a much stronger influence on the people of Chopwell than Marxism. Harry Bolton was never a card carrying member of the Communist Party and could only be described as a sympathiser or 'fellow traveller'. He strongly disagreed with the dictatorial and brutal aspects of the Soviet regime.

The Miners' Institute in the village was well-stocked with

Harry Bolton, leader of the Chopwell miners and a councillor, addresses a meeting in the 1920s. The Chopwell Lodge DMA banner, with its portraits of Keir Hardie, Marx and Lenin, forms a backdrop.

a wide range of books. The subjects included history, politics, philosophy, and religion, plus the classics of English literature. Another building housed the so-called 'Communist Club' which was founded for the study and discussion of political ideas. But Jack stresses that although most people who attended the club had socialist leanings, they were not necessarily communists. He says that the institute library and the 'Communist Club' radicalised the political thinkers of the village.

Two former colliery housing rows in Chopwell. Many of these rows survive in the village and are named after British rivers. This picture shows Humber Street.

Tom Yellowley

'These two catalysts together planted the seeds of, and set the scene for, 1926,' he adds.

Jack's grandfather arranged at one point for *The Northern Light* to be published from a caravan in Chopwell Woods. It was regarded by the authorities as a seditious publication. Local women were said to have hidden copies under their skirts if policemen were about.

Jack adds: 'When my grandfather and Will Lawther were tried at Gateshead court there was virtually a riot outside. Speaking of the six weeks or so that he spent in Durham Jail, my grandfather said the loud noise of the cell doors banging shut nearly drove him mad.' The police inspector who arrested Harry Bolton was disconcerted about doing so – he was arresting the chairman of the local magistrates. 'He said it was one of the hardest things he had ever had to do.'

Jack Fletcher also tells of a Chopwell vicar's son who, during the stoppage, went to work at the village colliery. Labelled a blackleg, he was booed and jeered by local people as he made his way home from the pit to the vicarage. 'The fact that he was a vicar's son gave him no special dispensation from having to run the gauntlet of the mining community's disapproval.'

The pit wheel memorial and heritage stone in Chopwell, which commemorate all those who worked at the village colliery 1896-1966.

Teacher Jack Fletcher stands beside Bolton's Bungalows, Chopwell, named after his grandfather Harry Bolton.

Chopwell was very much a typical pit village. A pall of sulphurous smoke from two large spoil heaps hung over the rows of colliery homes. The pit rows still survive and the streets are named after British rivers.

Former pitman Terry Meadows, also from Chopwell, says that during the dispute miners in the area stopped trains carrying coal. Their wives opened the doors under the trucks to get supplies for their home fires. 'They carried the coal away in their tin baths.' A police officer intent on catching those who raided coal stocks had all the coal taken from his own shed.

Terry, who worked at Chopwell, Hamsterley, Morrison Busty, Kibblesworth and Marley Hill collieries, comes from a family of miners, including his father, his father's brothers and his grandfather. He is chairman of Chopwell Band and Banner Committee and is proud of the area's socialist and mining heritage.

Terry was among those who believed that some sort of memorial to Chopwell's mining heritage should be sited in the village. A number of residents thought a pit wheel would be appropriate.

Former miner Terry Meadows.

Terry contacted former miner George Gill, then leader of Gateshead Borough Council, who agreed to help with the project. Terry then arranged for a large wheel to be sent up from Derbyshire. With aid from the Heritage Lottery Fund, the wheel, divided into two halves, together with a mining heritage stone, was erected in Derwent Street.

The stone bears lines from a Walt Whitman poem which are also on the Chopwell lodge banner: 'We take up the task eternal, the burden and the lesson. Pioneers! Oh! Pioneers!' The inscription also states: 'In honour of all those who worked at Chopwell Colliery 1896-1966.'

The General Strike remained solid. Large numbers of workers were clearly in sympathy with the miners. During this unprecedented national stoppage, volunteers recruited by the government drove buses and lorries. Volunteers also helped to keep the railways operating, but train services were greatly reduced. In Northumberland as well as Durham there were attempts by pickets to stop lorries transporting supplies and attacks, such as stone-throwing, on trams, buses and trains. There was deep resentment among the miners over the recruitment of the volunteer labour.

The most serious incident of obstruction occurred on May 10 on the East Coast main railway line when the famed Flying Scotsman passenger express was derailed a short distance to the south of Cramlington Station and north of the Damdykes level crossing. A rail had been removed from its position on the southbound track. The miners who carried out this sabotage had been trying to stop trains carrying coal. The Flying Scotsman had been their unintended and unexpected victim.

A number of passengers aboard the train were slightly hurt and one was more seriously injured, but fortunately the Flying Scotsman had been travelling at a low speed on this stretch of track. Mercifully, there were no fatalities, much to the relief of the miners who were aghast at what they had done. Eight men received jail sentences of between four and eight years as a result. They were all released after serving

5—JOURNAL AND NORTH STAR, FRIDAY, MAY 14, 1926.

CRAMLINGTON TRAIN WRECK.

A general view of the wrecked Scotch Express at West Cramlington, showing the engine lying on its side.

ncjMedia / The Journal

The Newcastle Journal reports the derailment at Cramlington. Mercifully, no one was killed.

less than four years. It seems one of these men was innocent of any involvement in the derailment.

Events in the General Strike moved rapidly to a conclusion. Despite the strong support for the miners, Baldwin's government would not give way. After nine days the TUC General Council called off the strike on May 12 following the unofficial intervention of Sir Herbert Samuel, chairman of the recent commission. He drew up a peace memorandum and held talks with the TUC, but his proposals did not have government backing. No promises were made by the government or employers to the TUC or the miners. Indeed, there were no pledges that men would be free from victimisation. The TUC General Council had accepted surrender on the basis of unofficial proposals. They were in a corner and saw Samuel's move as a way out.

Once more, the miners felt betrayed – this time by the TUC leaders. Despite this, they were heartened by the solid support received from their fellow workers throughout Britain. But they were now left to hold out alone, increasingly impoverished, for seven months. Miners and their families suffered great hardship during this period and soup kitchens for feeding the children were set up throughout the Great Northern Coalfield. At these improvised feeding stations they might be given cocoa, broth or sometimes other food, often provided by local farmers or shopkeepers. Miners' allotments and gardens were a source of vegetables.

Wives and children generally received totally inadequate relief payments from the local Boards of Guardians which administered the poor law. The men themselves were not entitled to any relief. Pitmen raided coal stocks at the mines or dug coal from outcrops to provide fuel for their home ranges.

Eventually, in late November 1926, the men had little alternative but to accept defeat and return to work for lower pay and longer hours. In both Durham and Northumberland the working shift underground was increased to eight hours plus one hour winding time, and the hours of hewers increased to seven and a half plus one hour winding time.

The Northumberland men had reluctantly voted to accept the owners' terms, but there was a final act of resistance by the miners of Durham. They voted by 49,217 to

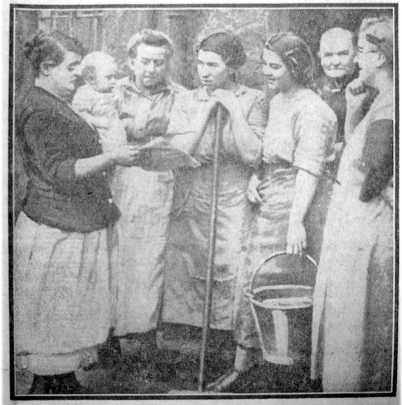

Wives of miners forsake their domestic duties for a few moments to discuss the news of the stoppage, which they will feel very keenly.

Newcastle Daily Chronicle May 3, 1926.

nciMedia / Evening Chronicle

40,583 to reject the terms. It was a result which showed that the fighting spirit of many pitmen had survived their ordeal. However, it was controversially ruled that a two thirds majority was required to continue the stoppage and this had not been achieved. The Durham men duly returned to work. They were among the last of Britain's miners to do so. After months of struggle and deprivation, it was a bitter pill to swallow.

Miners extinguishing their lamps during a coal strike—a significant picture. The present lock-out affects over a million miners.

Newcastle Daily Journal May 3, 1926.

Lads leading ponies out of a pit at the start of the strike. Some of the ponies had never before been above ground. Pictured in the Newcastle Daily Chronicle May 3, 1926.

ncjMedia / Evening Chronicle

ncjMedia / The Journal

The Bevin Boys

During the Second World War thousands of young men were conscripted to work in Britain's coal mines instead of the armed forces. They became known as the Bevin Boys, after wartime Minister of Labour Ernest Bevin, who introduced the scheme. They were selected by lots drawn at the offices of the ministry. Many did not come from mining areas, but they were needed underground as a large number of pitmen had joined the forces and there was a shortage of coal.

A few Bevin Boys stayed on at the pits after the war. Among them was Ron Harper, of Crawcrook, who had been brought up in Stoke Newington, London. In late 1943, Ron, who knew nothing about mining, was called to his local labour exchange in the capital and told to report for work in the North East coalfield. By early 1944, he was journeying by rail from King's Cross to Newcastle.

Ron was sent for training to the Morrison Busty Pit at Southmoor, Stanley, and afterwards did another spell of training at Greenside Colliery. He was then posted to Emma Colliery at Crawcrook. Ron married a Crawcrook girl and stayed on at the pit after the war. Following the closure of Emma, he transferred to Westoe at South Shields. Ron retired at the age of 60 in 1985 after the end of the miners' strike. By then he had worked in the North East pits for 42 years. That call to attend the labour exchange had changed the course of his life. Ron still has the carbide lamp he wore on his helmet at Emma, a memento of his life underground.

Bevin Boy Ron Harper stands at the pit wheel memorial marking the site of Emma Colliery, on the eastern edge of Crawcrook, where he worked for many years.

Tom Yellowley

Nationalisation of the mines

The nationalisation of Britain's coal mines under Clement Attlee's Labour government in 1947 ushered in a new epoch for the miners. Common ownership of the pits would mean they were run for the benefit of all the people. Leading this policy was Minister of Fuel and Power Emanuel Shinwell, MP for Seaham and, later, Easington. On Vesting Day, January 1 1947, the mines officially became the property of the whole of society rather than private companies. However, the miners did not share control of the pits with the newly-created National Coal Board as they had hoped.

Vesting Day was an occasion for celebration. The new NCB flag and the Union Flag flew from the tops of pithead towers throughout the region. There were parades, bands played in the colliery yards, speeches were made and the men were given a day's holiday, although essential maintenance and safety work still continued.

Ellington miner George Brown was then a member of Lynemouth Colliery Band and he remembers travelling to County Durham to play at a pit in the Washington area. 'It was a very special occasion, but a man was killed at this pit on Vesting Day and the celebrations were not so enthusiastic as they might have been.' The services of the band were also required that week at Ashington and Ellington collieries.

The NUM called upon the pitmen to increase productivity in a bid to meet high demand for coal and aid Britain's recovery from the damage wrought by the Second World War. The miners rose to the challenge. However, the country still had an overwhelming reliance on black diamonds for its source of energy and during the severe winter of 1946-47 there was a serious coal shortage.

Nationalisation meant that the way was now open for modernisation, but economic recovery was a slow process and modernisation correspondingly took a long time. Some pits in the North East were never converted to fully mechanised practices.

WE'RE NOW A NATION OF COALOWNERS To-day is Vesting Day. The mines now belong to YOU and the other 40 million Britons. Here is what two mining generations think of it.

ncjMedia / The Journal

Newcastle Daily Journal, January 1 1947.

Down the Algernon

'The floor was heaving and gas was hissing out …'
Jim 'Harry' Lucas

Jim 'Harry' Lucas, of North Shields, worked as a miner, deputy and ventilation officer in North Tyneside pits from 1947 to 1971. Following service during the Second World War in the Royal Navy, he joined the Algernon Pit as a trainee in 1947. The shafts of this mine were situated between New York and West Allotment about 50 yards behind a present-day car showroom premises. The upcast shaft of the colliery was known as the Kitty Pit and the downcast – for man-riding – was the Algernon Pit. There was a third shaft connected to the mine – the Prosperous Pit at Benton Square – which was used for ventilation and was available as an escape route in case of emergencies.

The Algernon was a relatively small colliery. The shafts went down to about 600ft. As a trainee Jim carried timber for pit props and girders to the face – there was only one pony at the mine so men were generally required to do these tasks. After a year, he joined the coalface and became a fully-fledged miner. He recalls that the working face was advanced between four and six feet each day. A cutter machine (like the one pictured on page 76) would undermine the coal and shot holes were drilled into the face every two yards. The deputy and shot-firers then moved in to set the explosives in the holes.

When the black diamonds had been blasted down they were broken up where necessary and shovelled on to a conveyor belt by the filler men. A series of conveyors took the coal to the main assembly point (known as a landing) from where it would fall into tubs operated by a rope haulage system which would take the coal to the shaft bottom. When it reached there, the onsetter, a man stationed at the foot of the shaft, would ensure that his team placed the tubs in the cage to be drawn to bank. The worker in charge at the surface end of the shaft was known as the banksman.

Jim recalls that the pit had one face which was particularly wet. They had to deal with vast amounts of water, so much that sometimes the coal was washed back on to the face. The walk to the face was a long one – sometimes as far as two miles.

After about two years as a face worker Jim applied to become a pit deputy, responsible for the safe management of a district in the workings. He passed his exams and seems to have enjoyed this job greatly.

As a deputy he carried a flame safety lamp which could be re-ignited if it went out. Unlike the rest of his team's lamps, the deputy's had a distinctive silver top. The flame on a deputy's lamp was turned down low and it was his job to use the lamp to test for the presence of firedamp. This he normally did by holding it near the roof, where methane, being lighter than air, was likely to accumulate. A blue cap would develop on the top of the flame if methane was present. This might take the form of a triangular halo and the flame might eventually go out. The changes observed in this 'cap' were crucial to determining the approximate level of gas.

In addition to the deputy, one in 10 miners would also carry a flame safety lamp – a glennie – for gas detection, although, unlike the deputy's, their lamps could not be immediately relit and were magnetically locked to avoid them being interfered with. If gas was present the flame would grow long and thin, eventually going out.

By this time, the brightness of the light provided by safety lamps had been improved. Each lamp was fitted with metal bars over the glass to prevent it breaking if knocked against the mine walls, dropped or hit by stones. From the late 1920s and 1930s onwards, miners also began wearing battery-operated electric lamps on their caps or helmets.

The traditional flame lamps, however, were vitally important. 'The safety lamp saved my life and the lives of the men many times,' says Jim. He recalls the time at Algernon when a Welsh miner, known as Taff, alerted him to the presence of firedamp coming from old workings. 'Taff told me that his lamp was out, the floor was heaving and gas was hissing out. Methane was pouring out of the floor. The gas had literally pushed the floor up.'

The mining operations had disturbed the fiery Bensham Seam of old workings in the closed Edward Pit, the shafts of which were in the area where the Tyne Metropolitan College now stands, close to the new Coast Road. These workings were below them. 'I pulled the lads out and sealed off the whole area,' says Jim. When he informed the manager of the danger he is said to have asked: 'Are you sure it's gas?' Jim had not a shred of doubt.

Blackdamp (another name for chokedamp) in which low levels of oxygen and high levels of carbon dioxide are present was another danger which he detected with his lamp. He remembers that while working with another deputy examining old workings he lowered his lamp and it went out.

Tom Yellowley

Veteran miner Jim 'Harry' Lucas, of Marden Farm Estate, North Shields, with his mel (pit hammer).

Blackdamp was present, which could potentially have put them at risk of suffocation, so they retreated from the area.

By the second half of the 20th century the hewer, the man who undercut the coal manually, had been superseded by the cutter machine operator, with teams of fillers loading the coal on to conveyors. The advent of shearers took things a step further – power loading meant that miners operated the shearer and moved the supports forward to advance the face.

Algernon, however, like many pits in the North East, never operated shearers and power loading. It retained the older method of cutter machine and blasting until closure. Jim tells of the changes which took place in the payment system for the men filling the coal onto conveyors: 'In the days of bord and pillar extraction each man attached his own number tally to the tub and the fillers were paid by the number of tubs they filled. The tubs were taken by a hand putter or pulled by a pit pony to the main ropeway or assembly point.

'With the advent of the coal cutting machine which undercut the coal seam and the introduction of conveyors to transport the coal to a main loading point or ropeway, a different, but simple, system of payment was evolved. For example, when a longwall face 200 yards long, by two feet six inches high was prepared a tender (claim) would be put out by a group of fillers based on a price per yard filled. When the face was filled off each shift they were allocated the full 200-yard price to be shared amongst them.' Men operating the coal cutting machines were paid according to the number of yards cut. The rates for both types of work were negotiated by the union.

In 1958 Jim Lucas suffered a crush injury to his spine when he was hit by a haulage cable in the pit. He was taken to the Tynemouth Jubilee Infirmary and was in plaster for around six months. Afterwards, he had a spell at the rehabilitation centre for injured miners at Hartford Hall, near Plessey Woods, Northumberland. The injury prompted him to apply for a job as ventilation officer at Algernon, in charge of ensuring a smooth airflow throughout the mine to expel gases.

He recalls his 19 years at Algernon with considerable warmth and knew most of the 600 men who worked there by name. They lived mainly at West Allotment, New York and North Shields. Nicknames were common in the pits and Jim was known to his fellow miners as 'Harry'.

Sadly, three men were killed during his time at Algernon, two by falls of stone and one in a transport accident.

Algernon closed in 1966 and Jim was transferred to the Rising Sun Colliery in the north of Wallsend where he was appointed chief ventilation officer. This was a much larger mine, employing around 1,700 men underground. Here it was impossible to know everyone's name.

In its last years the Rising Sun became a mechanised pit with shearer machines doing the extraction. It closed in 1969 and Jim played a key role in the team sent in to make the pit safe after the shutdown. Thus he found himself in the last cage out of the No 2 man-riding shaft before the job began of filling it in. No 1 shaft was also filled. Both were capped with metal girders and concrete. But the third shaft was kept open for a while to monitor the water levels in the mine.

As chief ventilation officer at the Rising Sun, it was Jim's job to ensure this large mine was free from any build-up of methane. 'The Sirocco electric fan was coarsing 375,000 cubic feet of air per minute through the workings,' he says.

Even so, Jim tells of the day when his work was challenged by a government mines inspector who had paid a surprise visit. 'I was told there was 2 per cent of methane in a roadway in the Brockwell.' It turned out that the inspector was using a new-style 'methaneometer' instead of a traditional glennie and he was pressing the wrong button, thus obtaining a misleading reading. Jim was able to put him right, and show the inspector there was no methane whatsoever in the roadway. The government official promptly dropped his complaint.

Among the lighter moments, Jim speaks of the day when he was told that men at one of the faces had 'struck gold'. They discovered a small cave amidst the coal which was 'flushed out with pyrites'. The glinting pyrites were found in an unusually abundant cluster and when a torch was shone on them they looked just like gold! 'It was like an Aladdin's cave.'

After the closure of the Rising Sun, Jim transferred to the Fenwick Pit near Earsdon. Its shafts were situated in the valley below Earsdon Church. This was a small mine, like the Algernon, worked by the older methods of cutter machine, blasting and wire rope haulage.

Some of the old Fenwick mine buildings

ncjMedia / The Journal

The Rising Sun Colliery, Wallsend, closed in 1969. Pictured are the four men in the last cage out of the pit on July 18, 1969. Front left, Jim 'Harry' Lucas, chief ventilation officer; front right, Harry Shand, onsetter; back left, Jim Pears, joiner; back right, Tommy Grindon, overman.

survive in the vicinity of the Earsdon to Backworth road. The Eccles, Maud, Fenwick and Algernon pits of North Tyneside were close together, and, before nationalisation, were part of the old Backworth Collieries Company. Some were connected to each other underground. The Eccles and Maud pits were only 200 hundred yards apart and were referred to jointly as Backworth Colliery. However they were separated by a geological fault which divided the two workings.

Jim worked as ventilation officer at Fenwick for a year, but in 1971 left for a change of direction. He trained to be a teacher and did 10 years at Walker Comprehensive School, Newcastle, before retiring.

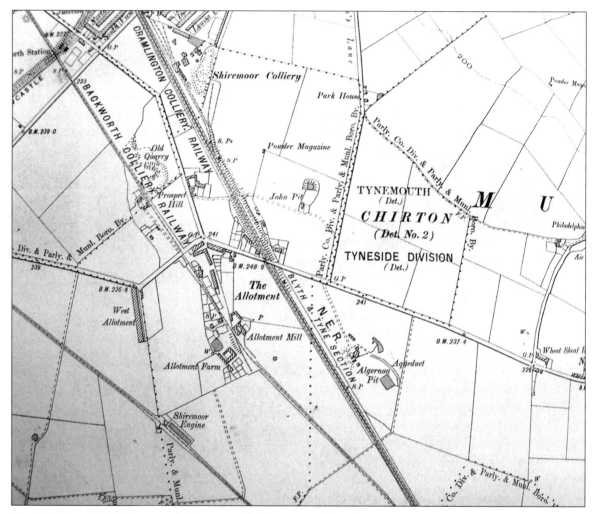

An OS Map of 1898 showing the location of Algernon Colliery between West Allotment and New York.

Wallsend Depths

'The quality of the High Main coals secured for them the premier place in the coal markets of the world.'
William Richardson, History of the Parish of Wallsend

Jim Lucas and his 'marras' – the North East pitman's term for his workmates – were taking part in the final stages of a long history of mining at Wallsend when they rode to bank in the last cage out of the Rising Sun. The area had once been famous for its top-quality coals which were highly valued throughout the world.

The era of mining in central Wallsend began in 1778 when work started on sinking a shaft – eventually known as the A Pit – a short distance west of the Segedunum Roman Fort and slightly south of the fort's West Gate. This was Wallsend Colliery's first shaft.

The project to sink the pit was initially led by William Chapman, a talented engineer with an inventive frame of mind. However, problems with water and quicksand were encountered and costs mounted. Soon the scheme was in financial difficulties and Chapman and his partners were forced to hand the uncompleted shaft and coal leases over to a creditor, William Russell senior, a merchant and financier.

Luck was on Russell's side, for the coal of the High Main seam was reached in 1781, a very short time after the unfortunate Chapman had withdrawn from the venture. The High Main was found at a depth of 600ft and the A Pit began production. Soon afterwards another shaft – the B Pit – was sunk close by, almost immediately north of the present day Buddle Street, again a little to the west of the fort and close to the line of Hadrian's Wall. Five additional shafts were sunk between 1786 and 1802, making a total of seven. These were the C, D, E, F and G pits.

The C Pit, also known as the Gas Pit, of Wallsend Colliery, engraved by Thomas Hair.

Another mine with a small colliery community developed in the late 18th century on the western fringes of Wallsend. The village became known as Bigges Main after landowner Thomas Bigge. The mine was abandoned in 1856 and the site is today occupied by part of Wallsend Golf Course.

The black diamonds won from Wallsend's High Main seam were of superb quality and fetched top prices on the world's markets. Indeed, coal from other areas was sometimes sold under the name 'Wallsend' in an attempt to make more profit.

At first using horses and the force of gravity, but later sometimes using steam locomotive power, the coal was transported the short distance from the town's pits to the staiths on the banks of the Tyne where it was loaded into keels or collier ships. It was boom time for William Russell senior and his descendants, Matthew and William junior. Russell senior became a very wealthy man.

However, by 1831 the High Main was virtually exhausted and afterwards coal was mined from another seam, the Bensham, 200ft below. It was the fiery nature of this seam which led to the disastrous explosion of 1835 in which 102 lives were lost. During this era the viewer, or manager, of the colliery was John Buddle junior, a man who encouraged Sir Humphry Davy to develop his safety lamp and who worked on improving ventilation of mines, but not, it seems, with great success.

Despite the 1835 pit disaster and other tragedies involving loss of life,

mining continued at Wallsend for nearly 20 more years. But by this time the colliery's profits had fallen considerably. The Bensham seam proved much less lucrative than the High Main since its coal was suitable mainly for gas making, but the gas industry was at an early stage of development. With profits dwindling, William Russell junior pulled out of mining in the area towards the end of 1847. The next year new owners took over the colliery.

The first phase of 19th century mining in Wallsend came to a dramatic end which saw the town's coals absent from the market for nearly 50 years. Between 1854 and 1859 nearly all the mines of the mid-Tyne area, both north and south of the river, were overwhelmed by floodwater and forced to close. These included Wallsend, which in 1854 was one of the first to cease production as water poured relentlessly into the workings.

Friars Goose pumping engine painted by Thomas Hair in the 1840s.

The owners of the Wallsend, Willington, Heaton, Walker, and Felling collieries had come to an agreement in 1843 that they would pay the owners of the Friars Goose Colliery, on the eastern fringes of Gateshead, to use a powerful pumping engine to keep down the level of water affecting the mid-Tyne area. However, it was found that water could be held back from seeping downwards into a pit by lining the upper part of a shaft with iron 'tubing'. After installing the tubing, some of the owners decided they could save money by pulling out of the agreement and the Friars

Goose pumping engine ceased operating in 1851. However, the pressure of water proved too strong and the tubing gave way. The only pit in the mid-Tyne area where the tubing held was Walker. The first mine to be 'drowned out' was Jarrow, which had no tubing at all.

Not until 1866 did work start on re-opening Wallsend Colliery. Those involved must have known that pumping the water from the mine would be an immense and lengthy task. Pumping engines were set up at the G Pit and operations began on sinking a new shaft, the H, less than 100 yards away.

The pumping work lasted a long time at both the G and H shafts, but gradually the water level was greatly lowered. This helped to reduce the level in some of the other collieries in the Mid-Tyne area, but Wallsend remained closed because its owners concentrated on resuming mining at Hebburn.

Coal was too valuable a commodity to waste. The Wallsend and Hebburn Coal Company was formed in 1893 and one of its aims was to restart production at Wallsend. This goal was achieved in 1897 when the first coals were drawn from the new H Pit. During the following year the G Pit started production again.

The G and H pits of the colliery were very close together on land immediately to the west of today's Hadrian Road Metro Station and immediately to the east of Waggon Way, being bordered to the north by the Metro line. The G and H pits closed in the 1930s.

Tom Yellowley

The ruins of the old Friars Goose pumping engine house, near the Tyne at Gateshead.

In 1908 the Wallsend and Hebburn Coal Company opened another mine in the area north of the Coast Road. This was the Rising Sun Colliery, named after a local farm. Work began on sinking the first shaft to the Bensham seam in 1906. The mine was to become one of the largest on Tyneside and by the early 1960s employed around 2,000 men, with 1,700 of these underground.

It Seemed Like Another World

'I often wonder where they all are, and I think of our times together.'
Norman Lindsay

Norman Lindsay, of Wallsend, began work as a trainee surveyor at the Rising Sun Colliery in 1940 at the age of 14, but after only three months had to leave when his family moved to Shilbottle in Northumberland. His father had been a deputy at the Rising Sun and was taking up a similar position at the Shilbottle mine.

After serving in the Army during the Second World War, Norman rejoined the workforce at the Rising Sun in 1948, this time as a trainee pitman. He remembers Vesting Day that year when Britain's mines were officially nationalised. To mark the transfer of the Rising Sun from private to public ownership a Union Jack was flown from the pithead winding gear.

Norman writes: 'In March 1948 after being demobbed I came to Wallsend. I decided to get a job with the Rising Sun Colliery. I had previously been employed there at the age of 14.

I started work on the day shift with two marras. We were employed as timber leaders. I was very apprehensive on my first day, but my worries were unfounded. As far as my workmates were concerned I couldn't have done better.

The Rising Sun Colliery, in the northern area of Wallsend, in the 1960s.

'After entering the pithead baths I left my clean clothes in the clean locker and walked past the shower with my towel around my waist, and changed into my pit clothes on the dirty locker side. Then everyone would leave the baths to collect their lamps and identity discs. I met my marras at the shaft top and we went down together to the Three Quarter Seam. Emerging from the cage seemed like entering another world, and it took some time to get accustomed to. On the way inbye we collected our pony from the stables. He was all black and named Jackie, and we were all greatly attached to him.'

Norman was to stay at the Rising Sun for five years and comments: 'Our work down the mine kept us all fit. It was a hard life but I have no regrets at having lived it that way. True friendship counted a lot, and still does, in this world. I often wonder where they all are, and I think of our times together.'

Ray Grew worked at the Rising Sun from 1964 until its closure in 1969, after which he stayed on for a while to help carry out salvage operations. Ray still lives close to the site of the mine. He started at the age of 16 as a trainee, serving at first, like Norman, in the transport section and eventually progressing to become a face worker.

Ray's work in transport involved taking timber pit props and sometimes girders to the men extracting the coal. These were transported in tubs or trams, and were often pulled by the mine's numerous pit ponies, known to the men as Gallowas (a reference to the old Galloway breed of pony).

There were two working seams in the Rising Sun at this time, the Brockwell and the Beaumont, and each had its own underground stables for the ponies. The two stables were whitewashed and included an area for grooming. Each stable housed around 30 ponies. Every one of these magnificent little animals had its own stall. They spent most of their lives

Richard Smith

Vanished pit. Former miner Ray Grew stands at the site of one of the Rising Sun Colliery's shafts, now capped and grassed over.

underground, but were sometimes brought to the surface.

'I remember the ponies sometimes being brought up from the pit and taken to stables above ground on the site of the Edward Pit, where the Tyne Metropolitan College building at Battle Hill is today,' says Ray. The Edward Pit was an old one which had reopened for production in 1913. This area was used as a training ground for the ponies.

In August 1925 the Edward Pit was hit by tragedy when five miners, two under the age of 20, were killed as a result of an explosion. It was thought that the blast was caused by a spark from a coal-cutter machine coming into contact with unexpected methane.

The ponies pulled the tubs carrying the props and girders during Ray's time at the Rising Sun, although until the early 1960s they were also used to haul coal. Norman Lindsay says that many people believed that the pit ponies were blind, but this was untrue. They were able to see, but when brought to the surface their eyes took a little while to adjust to the light.

Norman recalls the pit ponies and the wire rope haulage system: 'There were continuously running ropes and the set of tubs were attached to them by means of a steel clip at each end of the set. In the Three Quarter Seam stable, which also housed the ponies for the Brockwell Seam, the ponies were fastened in separate stalls and had a horse keeper to take care of their needs.'

The ponies were also employed on some of the loaders. 'At the end of the coal shift the belts would be running empty and they would jump on with their handlers for a free ride outbye. They jumped off when approaching low points and back on again when all was safe.'

Norman adds: 'Ponies were also used in the main coal seam, which was worked 'bord and wall'. The putters would ride on the limbers behind the ponies, taking empty tubs to

Richard Smith

A miner's flame safety lamp from the Rising Sun Colliery. Such lamps were vital for gas detection.

the fillers from the inbye landings and bringing back the full ones. This was extremely heavy work for both putters and ponies. They were also used to pull tubs of stone out on the stonework shift.'

He recalls: 'Every pony, just like people, had its own characteristics. Most of them were very placid, whilst others would try and bite or lash out at their handlers. These ones had to be handled with care. Others would run back to the stables at the first opportunity with the handler in hot pursuit and shouting words of endearment after it. Bait had to be carefully guarded from them and the men usually carried it in tins. But the ponies would be given titbits by their handlers. Some would even chew tobacco.'

It seemed these sturdy little animals could sense danger. 'It has been known for a pony to stop for no apparent reason and shortly afterwards there would be a fall of roof,' declares Norman.

For many years the Rising Sun had two shafts, No 1 and No 2. In the early 1960s a third shaft was sunk, very much wider than the other two and around 1,200ft to 1,300ft deep. The No 3 was used to draw coals to the surface. By this time No 1 was used mainly for ventilation and No 2 (around the same depth as No 3) for the men. The deepest seam being worked at this time was the Brockwell, reaching a depth of perhaps 1,400ft. The coal was taken away from the pit by trains.

'The Rising Sun was a fairly gaseous mine,' says Ray, 'and in its south-east and south-west sections it was wet. In the south-east area there were roadways which might contain water up to six inches deep and water leaked from the roofs.

Tina Job collection

Eddie Job junior, second left, and his marras enjoy a carefree moment at bank at the Rising Sun in the 1960s (see page140).

In some places the effect was like a bathroom shower! To the north conditions were much drier.' Some of these roadways ran beneath Wallsend High Street 'In fact, there are mine tunnels under much of the town.'

It was possible for a miner to go on an underground walk from the Rising Sun workings to the tunnels of the old G Pit, a distance of around two miles. Ray sometimes did this walk when he worked in the ventilation section. There were said to be about 50 miles of tunnels beneath the area.

The closed G Pit was no longer producing coal, but a pumping station was installed at the bottom of the shaft to keep the water levels down in the Rising Sun workings. The old pit cage and wheel were still in place to enable maintenance to be carried out. Instead of walking along the underground roadways Ray sometimes descended the G shaft in the cage. The nearby H shaft, barely 40 yards away, was used for upcast ventilation and also for pumping purposes.

From near the bottom of the G Pit one of the tunnels sloped downwards towards the River Tyne. Ray noted that on old colliery maps it was marked as the 'Hebburn Roadway'. He explored this tunnel but found that after 50 to 100 yards a dam blocked any further progress. It was holding back water. Did this roadway once lead under the Tyne to link up with the workings of the old Hebburn Colliery?

Jim 'Harry' Lucas, the last chief ventilation officer at the Rising Sun, was able to provide the answer. 'My ventilation plans showed three roadways, very close together, linking the G Pit with Hebburn Colliery, no doubt in the days of the Wallsend and Hebburn Coal Company. These roads were dammed off and became the sump for the G Pit pumping station.'

The possibility of danger was ever present. Ray Grew remembers many times seeing the flashes of light as he worked at the coal face with a shearer machine. Such frictional sparks might be dangerous if methane was present, but fortunately the mine was well ventilated.

Ray tells of a man being killed by a roof collapse while working at the face in the Brockwell seam only a few months before the closure of the Rising Sun in April 1969. He also remembers a fatal accident with a shearer machine a few years earlier and that a pumping station man at the G Pit was killed by an explosion (caused by an unexpected build-up of methane from old workings) in the early 1960s.

Colin Finlay, of the High Farm Estate, Wallsend, also lives near the colliery site. He worked at the mine for around five years, starting as a trainee in 1955 at the age of 15. 'We were always singing. The song with the words 'You load 16 tons' was particularly popular. We would sing down the mine and as we were being drawn up and down the shaft in the cage.'

Colin recalls the water problem in some parts of the workings; the Brockwell seam in particular was noted for its dampness. 'I've seen men doubled up, half submerged in water as they shovelled the coal'.

The Rising Sun had a reputation as a hot pit. 'It was very warm. Men would often work in just their shorts,' says Colin. Indeed, it was so warm that on one occasion Ray Grew and some of his marras fell asleep while on night shift. When they did not appear at bank a search party was sent out for them. They were discovered safe and well, but they had been asleep for several hours!

The Welfare Field, off Kings Road North, Wallsend, was where the miners played football and other sports. It is opposite the former colliery entrance at the northern end of the road. The field was also used for the popular sport of whippet racing.

With the colliery's demise a way of life which had lasted for two centuries vanished, although smoke still seeped from the coaly ground above the mine for many years afterwards, a reminder of even more coaly times past. The site of the Rising Sun Colliery is today a country park, managed by North Tyneside Council. The capped shafts are grassed over. Three slag or spoil heaps which once dominated the scene have been landscaped and remodelled into two pleasant hills. Visitors stroll happily above the perilous depths where men once laboured far below.

Beneath the Sea

'When my clothes dried they were covered in salt.'
Malcolm Barras

Ray Grew was far from finished with mining when he left the Rising Sun. After a seven-year stint at the Eccles Pit at Backworth, he transferred to Westoe Colliery at South Shields in 1980 and stayed until the pit closed.

The Westoe mine extended out under the North Sea for several miles. Some of the workfaces were seven miles or more from the shaft bottom, many being roughly parallel to the coast. Westoe was not the only such mine. Important collieries operated along the entire coast of County Durham, including Wearmouth, Vane Tempest, Easington, Horden, Dawdon and Blackhall. The shafts of these mines went down through the magnesian limestone which overlays the coal seams in eastern Durham.

At Westoe, Ray had a particularly frightening experience while he was carrying out inspection duties as a deputy. He was checking an old roadway when his safety lamp 'blew' and went out. The small explosion inside the lamp had been caused by methane. 'There was literally no air. I couldn't breathe. It was very frightening'. He quickly retreated from the area. A short time later he advanced again and put his lamp towards the affected spot to check the gas. It was almost certainly coming from old workings, seeping through damaged partitioning.

Before nationalisation in 1947, the Harton Coal Company of South Shields owned St Hilda, Harton, Boldon and Whitburn (Marsden) collieries. St Hilda was the oldest

Tom Yellowley

Top, *the site of St Hilda Colliery today. The rear section of this building houses a shaft, which in its last working years was used for ventilation and emergency exit purposes for Westoe Colliery. The warning sign below survives in the building.*

mine, dating to 1825 when sinking was completed (see page 45). The company opened Westoe as a shaft of the St Hilda Colliery in 1909. St Hilda closed in 1940, but the Westoe shaft was reopened in 1947 for drawing coal and a shaft at St Hilda was brought back into use for ventilation and as an emergency exit.

Westoe was now developed as a colliery in its own right. Only a short distance from the seafront at South Shields, the mine was ideally situated to exploit the coal reserves beneath the waves.

In the 1950s a second shaft for Westoe was opened, the Crown, which was mainly used for coal drawing, with the Westoe Shaft concentrating on man-riding. The three-tier Westoe cage was capable of carrying up to 150 men, 50 on each tier. The Crown Shaft was equipped with a huge skip for coal, but could also accommodate around 20 men in a smaller cage.

Today, new housing, known as Westoe Crown Village, has been built on the site of the mine. Its streets are named after areas of the colliery, including Sea Winnings Way, Greenside Drift and Brass Thill Way, recalling the Brass Thill Seam. A fenced-off area on the edge of the development is the site of the Crown Shaft. The base of the tower and the concrete cap over the shaft are clearly visible. Two pipes protrude from the cap to release any remaining gas.

The Harton Coal Company had its own private railway lines which took the coal from its pits to Harton Staiths at South Shields. The company's trucks were painted a distinctive red and much of the network

was electrified in 1908 using locomotives built by Siemens in Berlin. For many years there were two sets of staiths, the Harton High and the Harton Low, with the Low Staiths, next to Mill Dam, surviving the longest.

The company's track from Westoe to Whitburn Colliery became known as the Marsden Rattler route and this remained a steam line. It carried passengers as well as coal trains. The name 'Rattler' was a reference to the noisy and shaky second-hand carriages used on this well-loved coastal track. Regular passenger services ended in 1953, although the coal trains continued until 1968 when Whitburn Colliery closed.

Most of the village of Marsden was built immediately to the north of Souter Lighthouse to accommodate Whitburn Colliery miners and their families. The pit was a short

International Maritime

Whitburn Colliery, c1900. A coal train is pictured on the right. To the left is the 'Marsden Rattler' passenger train.

distance to the south of the lighthouse, between the main South Shields-Sunderland road and the sea. Its twin shafts went down to a depth of 1,700ft. Two rows of houses, formerly owned by the colliery, survive on the other side of the road, the rear one named Arthur Street. They faced the shafts.

The first buildings in the main part of Marsden village to the north were constructed in around 1874, the year the pit opened, and the settlement grew to nine streets, 136 houses and a population of around 600-700. The village also had allotments, a school, Co-op store, post office and Miners' Institute. A chapel building still survives, to the south of the lighthouse, on the western side of the main road. Also to the south, on the eastern side, was the Welfare Field.

All signs of the main community to the north have now vanished. Its houses and streets were demolished following closure of the pit and the site is now a grassed area overlooking the sea. The residents moved to Whitburn and other nearby areas. Not all the miners, however, lived in this now lost community. Some travelled to work from South Shields via the 'Rattler'.

Malcolm Barras, of Simonside, South Shields, trained as a mechanical fitter at Whitburn Colliery, working there from 1963 to 1968. The original name for the mine was Marsden Colliery, but it was re-named Whitburn because of possible confusion with Marden Colliery in Yorkshire.

The Whitburn Lodge pub, on the eastern side of the main

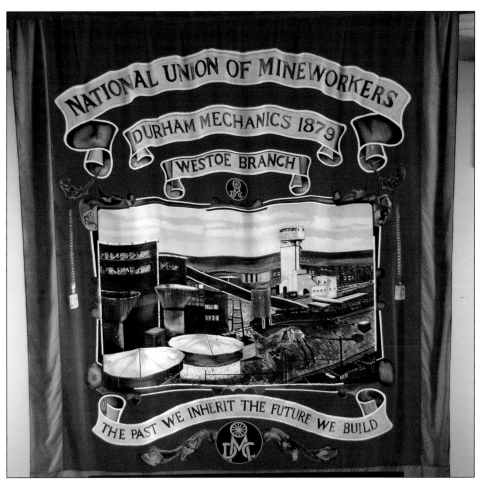

Tom Yellowley

The banner of Westoe Branch of the Durham Mechanics, which is today on display at St Hilda's Church, South Shields. The illustration on the banner shows Westoe Colliery.

road, was the colliery manager's house and the entrance to the pub car park is flanked by stone pillars, each bearing the emblem of a miner's helmet and depicting a shovel and pick. 'The pillars are the original ones marking the entrance to the colliery,' Malcolm told the authors. 'The car park was the pit yard.'

Whitburn Colliery passenger station was next to the entrance. Miners travelling from South Shields on the Rattler could step from the station straight into the colliery. Coal trains from the pit joined the route a short distance north of the station. A stone pillar of the old railway bridge, which carried the coal trucks across the road, still stands close to Souter Lighthouse

No 1 and No 2 shafts are now filled in and capped. The site of No 2 shaft is marked by a cluster of trees and shrubs in a shallow depression close to the sea. No 1 shaft was next to what is now the pub car park, and is marked by a small, grassed mound surmounted by a beacon brazier. A covered footbridge stretched across the road from the mine's lamp cabin to pithead baths on the western side.

Malcolm still has a brass identity token, carrying his number, from his mining days. 'You picked up your two identity tokens from the lamp cabin, one silver-coloured and the other brass. Before entering the cage you handed the silver token to the banksman but kept the brass one. This was handed in when you reached bank at the end of your shift.'

Malcolm considers himself lucky. During his 25 years working underground he only suffered a broken finger and 'tons of cuts and bruises' but no major accidents. Others were unlucky and, he tells of a man who lost an arm when it

Tom Yellowley

Former pit mechanic Malcolm Barras, of South Shields, with his identity token at the gates of Whitburn Colliery, now the entrance to the Whitburn Lodge pub car park.

was caught in the mechanism of a conveyor belt at Whitburn.

Working conditions could be wet: 'The colliery extended for up to three miles out to sea. When my clothes dried out at home they were covered in salt.' His job was to maintain and repair a wide variety of machinery, including pumps and pipework and equipment at the longwall faces. He worked on servicing trepanners, machines which were a cross between the old coal-cutters and modern shearers. The men rode towards the face on electric trains. There were no ponies used at Whitburn during Malcolm's time, but they had been employed in the past and the stables were still there, a reminder of a less mechanised era.

Malcolm's wife, Dorothy, comes from a mining family stretching back several generations. Her grandfather and three uncles worked at Whitburn. They lived in Chichester, South Shields, in the days when there were no pithead baths. They shared a tin one. Her grandmother's life was a continual round of heating water, washing and cooking for her husband and sons, who were frequently on different shifts and needed to bath and be fed at all times of the day. The eldest daughter did not go out to work but helped her mother in the house. As the girls married and left home the next daughter in line took up this task. Later, one of the uncles moved to a house opposite the colliery. When the wind was blowing in from the sea the coal dust made it difficult to keep things clean.

Dorothy told her grandad that she thought it was cruel to keep the pit ponies working so hard underground, but he argued 'It's a better life than some of them have up-top'.

Following closure of Whitburn in 1968 a great deal of machinery was abandoned beneath the seabed. Malcolm transferred to Westoe, a relatively short distance to the north. This mine employed the most modern methods; shearers were the norm. The Westoe man-riding shaft was 1,300ft deep with undeveloped reserves at the bottom. The mine was being worked at the 623ft and 923ft levels, drifting down to the 1,350ft level.

Malcolm was a member of Westoe Lodge of the Durham Mechanics union, affiliated to the NUM. The lodge banner (see page 107), with its picture of the Crown shaft and coal washer plant is on display at St Hilda's Church.

Also in South Shields was Harton Colliery, which began

production in the 1840s and closed in 1969. It was sited off Harton Lane, between South Tyneside District Hospital and Boldon Lane, flanked to the south by John Reid Road. As is so often the case, today there is no sign this pit ever existed. Its entrance was on the western side of the present-day junction of The Wynde and Harton Lane.

A few miles inland from Whitburn lies Boldon Colliery, a village named after its mine, which once featured an attractive Miners' Hall. The Boldon pit was located immediately to the north east of North Road, a street flanked by terraced rows of little colliery houses, still occupied, with long, narrow front gardens. At one time there were around 500 similar homes in the village. The entrance to the pit was on the eastern side of North Road, close to its junction with Hedworth Lane and near the Colliery Tavern.

A fine semi-circle of Aged Miners' Homes stands less than half a mile away, near the junction of Hedworth Lane and Abingdon Way. Another group of homes, dated 1928, is opposite. Even nearer the junction is a row of tubs, a

Richard Smith

Homes at Boldon Colliery built by the Durham Aged Mineworkers' Homes Association.

reminder of the area's long mining history. Boldon Colliery closed in 1983. Like a considerable number of North East pits, it had lasted well over 100 years.

Keith Jones, of Cleadon, knew Boldon Colliery well – he worked there as a miner, deputy and overman. Indeed, his father was a fore-overman at the pit and the family lived in a colliery-owned house next to the mine. Keith began his training as an apprentice electrician, attending Dame Margaret Hall at Washington for instruction in underground work. But at the age of 18 he decided to become a miner rather than an electrician.

Because his father was a fore-overman in one part of the Boldon pit, Keith generally worked in the other part. However, there were times during holidays when his father would be responsible for the whole mine and to avoid the charge of favouritism he gave his son some of the tougher jobs! It was by no means any easy lot being the son of an official.

Keith did most jobs in the pit, eventually becoming a coal-cutter at the face. It was while working in this front-line position that he suffered a back injury in a roof fall. His father had suffered a similar accident 23 years earlier and was off work for about three months. Keith, whose injury was less severe, managed to return after five or six weeks. His pit career was far from over and he progressed to become a deputy and then an overman as well as joining the mines rescue brigade.

As a boy, Keith displayed a great talent for drawing and at the age of 12 or 13 he was drafted in at Boldon Colliery to draw damaged pit tubs and bent girders which had been involved in underground accidents and then brought to the surface. His father explained the circumstances of an accident to him and Keith produced sketches to help

Stafford Linsley

Boldon Colliery, 1968.

investigators understand how it happened.

His talents were clearly appreciated and while a miner he began drawing colourful cartoon-style safety posters for the National Coal Board. These posters were displayed at collieries throughout Britain to warn miners of dangers and remind them of the necessary safety procedures. In his spare time Keith drew cartoons for national newspapers including the *Daily Mirror*, *The News of the World*, *The Sun* and other papers and he became a member of the Cartoonist Club of Great Britain.

Calligraphy is another of Keith's talents. He produced a memorial citation to the 100 miners killed in accidents or who died of natural causes at Boldon Colliery. The first casualty was an unknown boy. The citation and list of names is displayed at St Nicholas Church in Boldon. There is another copy next to the Boldon miners' banner at the village's North Road Social Club, known as 'The Shack'.

Keith explains that colliery-owned houses were low rent or rent free. They were gradually sold off by the National Coal Board and miners were given first refusal to buy.

Because Boldon Colliery was a 'trial' mine for all types of new machinery, it was not set a production target as other pits were. Keith's experience with the new equipment led to him becoming a mechanisation demonstrator for the North Durham Area in the 1960s. He visited pits throughout the district to give instruction and install the new machinery, including shearers, Joy loaders and trepanners, then his responsibility was extended to the South Durham Area.

He eventually returned to Boldon with the task of attempting to get 1,000 tons of coal per shift off a longwall face. This had never been done before. Using Panza conveyors and two AB disc shearers, he and his team were very successful – they achieved 1,300 tons per shift.

Later he was promoted to the position of NCB mine stones executive, responsible for the sale and disposal of pit heaps following mine closures. Some of the material was used in road construction. The Aberfan disaster had triggered a drive to get rid of spoil 'mountains' .

As a senior official, Keith did not forget his mining days or his marras. Seeing men on the picket line during the 1984-85 strike reminded him that 'There but for the grace of God go I.' He took flasks of tea and coffee to the pickets and gave miners some of his free coal allocation. He was unhappy to see the way the pitmen were treated. Today, Keith still keeps his old safety lamp and a bait tin on top of a display cabinet at his home, a reminder of his time served at Boldon Colliery.

Tom Yellowley

Former Boldon Colliery miner Keith Jones, of Cleadon, with one of his mine safety posters.

The Garage Colliery

'Yes, I'm a pitman.'
Roger Harrison

Former miner Roger Harrison, of Whitley Bay, remembers his 12 years at Shilbottle Colliery in Northumberland and his marras at the pit with obvious affection. He proudly declares 'Yes, I'm a pitman.' His private garage at Whitley Bay is something of a museum as Roger has installed models representing a working pit. There is a replica of a mine tunnel with a pony pulling tubs and even a man working as a hand putter. 'Where the roof was too low for ponies, a man would have to push the tubs,' comments Roger.

There are two model pit shafts, one complete with a cage which moves up and down. A replica tunnel shows two pitmen riding in tubs, pulled by a cable operated by electric motor in Tommy Swordy's 'haala hoose' (hauler house). The model men in the tubs represent two of Roger's marras, Geordie Douglas and Kenny Wilcox. Roger also rode inbye from the shaft in this way.

Yet another model shows the 'tippler' house on the surface where the tubs of coal from the pit were tipped over to fall down a chute onto the screens, a conveyor belt arrangement where rubble, stones and other debris, such as broken pit props, were manually removed from the coal before it journeyed downwards into coal waggons standing on a track running beneath the screens building. From there the loaded waggons would be pulled away from the mine by a tank engine, known to all miners as a 'tanky'. Every mine, of course, had its tippler and screens and the removal of the debris was known as 'picking'.

Pickers work on the screens at Hazlerigg Colliery, near Wideopen, while bowler-hatted officials inspect the proceedings c1919.

Roger says: 'I started at Shilbottle Colliery as a picker on the screens at the age of 15 in 1950-51. Joe Nicholson, one of the screen workers, told me that we were "film stars". Why? Because we worked on the screens.'

He attended Ashington Mining School as a trainee before going underground at Shilbottle and becoming a face worker. The seam at this pit, the 'Shilbottle' seam, a few miles to the south of Alnwick, was a thin one, only 27 inches high in places. It was worked by cutter machine and blasting, the usual method in the 1950s.

Roger lived at Bilton Banks, a tiny village a relatively short distance to the north-east of Shilbottle. The cottages there have now been demolished and there is nothing left of the homes in Long Row and Short Row (pronounced 'Raa') where he grew up. Roger lived in Long Row. There was no running water in these cottages. It all had to be got from a standpipe outside and carried indoors. There was no electricity either. Roger's family used paraffin lamps. Outside were netties – earth toilets. These homes had originally been constructed for miners who worked at the Longdyke pit, on the edge of Bilton Banks. This mine closed in 1924 and many of the pitmen in the village then transferred to the nearby Shilbottle or Whittle collieries.

A shaft of the old pit was covered over with a steel grill and as a boy Roger and his friends would dare each other to walk over it. 'I did it – but only once.' They would drop stones down the shaft and wait a long time before they heard them crashing at the bottom. The depth terrified them.

Roger worked at Shilbottle and his father at Whittle. 'The water from the standpipe was heated on the kitchen range and when we returned from work we had to use the same tin bath. The last man in did not have the cleanest of baths!' jokes Roger. There were no pithead baths at Shilbottle until

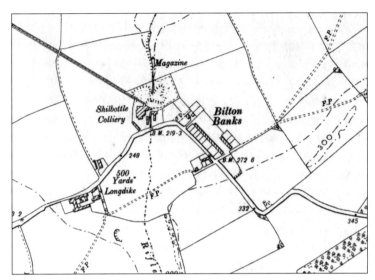

An Ordnance Survey Map of 1898 showing the tiny village of Bilton Banks, comprising two rows of houses, and the site of part of Shilbottle Colliery, known as the Longdyke Pit. This pit closed before Roger Harrison was born. He worked in another section of Shilbottle Colliery which closed in 1982.

his final years there.

He and his family did eventually move to Shilbottle, but he still recalls those days at Bilton Banks with fondness. He speaks of the delicious rabbit pies which his mother made. 'She made the best rabbit pie in Bilton Banks. There were five of us – myself, my father, brother, mother and sister. And we all got one leg, even though a rabbit only has four!'

Roger was to go on to become an inventor. He started by designing and patenting systems for preventing moving and trailing cables used in mines from becoming snared or tangled. The most important of these was the Relhco Cable Slide for controlling cables supplying power to coal shearer machines at the face. Another of his inventions was an interlocking design for spill plates to prevent coal from falling off conveyor belts at the face. Roger went on to set up a business to market his devices.

In his model colliery there is a replica of a longwall face and a model shearer machine which moves along it. Roger describes how the shearer extracts coal from the face by means of tungsten picks attached to a revolving drum, and the coal falls onto the conveyor belt.

Shearer machines came to be adopted in the largest, most modern of the North East's mines although the older methods of cutter machine and blasting were still being used in many of the region's pits until their closure.

On one of the shelves in Roger's garage is a 'Self-Rescuer'. This is a breathing device which a miner carried in case of carbon monoxide – the lethal afterdamp following explosions. The 'Self-Rescuer' filters out the deadly fumes, keeping the miner alive for perhaps 20 minutes or so. But Roger stresses that any pitman cut off from reaching fresh air would be unlikely to survive after this time had elapsed.

Also on a wall are several small-sized model safety lamps. 'If a blue cap developed and then the flame went out you would head for the shaft.' One of Roger's uncles died as the result of an explosion at Shilbottle between the world wars.

The mine closed in 1982. The best coal had by then been extracted. Today the site has been cleared and grassed over, except for the main office block and manager's house, which are now private homes.

Roger Harrison left Shilbottle Colliery many years ago, but his thoughts are still with his marras and his experiences under the surface of Northumberland.

Former Shilbottle miner Roger Harrison stands beside part of the model colliery in his garage.

Ponies and Men

'We wore babies' nappies as neckerchiefs.'
John Douds

John Douds, of Seaton Sluice, worked for 30 years in the pits of South East Northumberland, once a stronghold of mining. He comes from a mining family stretching back generations; his father was a pony putter and his grandfather was killed at Seghill Colliery by a fall of stone.

His early years were spent at Seaton Delaval but the family later moved to Bedlington where his father had found work at the colliery. Before the move, and while John was still a young boy, his father would take him on the bus from Seaton Delaval to Bedlington on pay day. John's mother needed the money that day. Luckily his grandmother lived near the colliery and she would put the pay packet in John's top pocket and sew the pocket up. John was then put on the bus back to Seaton Delaval. His mother met him when the bus arrived and unpicked the stitches. 'I was aged only about four at the time,' he says.

At the age of 15, John began work as a trainee at Bedlington A Pit. He went to Ashington Mining School, as all trainees did in those days, and then, when he reached 16, began work underground.

Bedlington A went down to nearly 1,000ft in its deepest seam, the Denton Low Main or Tilley. At this mine he first began working with ponies. John became a 'pony leader' or 'timber leader', taking girders, timbers and other supplies to the face. There were around 35 ponies in the underground stables at this time, although he was told by old hands that many years before there had been around 200.

As well as taking supplies into the pit, the ponies were also used to haul loaded tubs from the face. The largest were employed on the main roadways. This was a really traditional mine, as were so many in the North East.

After four years at Bedlington A John moved to Bates Colliery in Blyth. This was close to the southern bank of the town's harbour. He had been sent to this pit to do face training, but then Bedlington A closed and so John stayed on at Bates. He stayed there for 15 years and became a face worker. John went on to work as a hydraulic fitter at the mine, repairing and maintaining roof supports. This pit had been an extension of the old Cowpen Colliery (pronounced by the miners as 'Coopen') the shafts of which were very close to those of Bates. The workings of the two mines were linked. Cowpen's first shaft dated to the late 18th century.

The Three Quarter Seam district of Bates was very wet. John and his marras wore oilskins, gloves, wellingtons and waders;, they must have looked like seamen. 'We wore babies' nappies as neckerchiefs to stop the water from the roof seeping down our necks,'. The water was salty – Bates extended out to sea. 'You never shaved before you went to work, as if you did the salty water brought your face out in a red rash.' Underfoot, the floor was 'claggy' with a mud which gave off a salty smell. Conditions were uncomfortable – there were occasions when he would have to lie on his side with water dripping in his ear.

Later John moved to Ashington Colliery, where he

worked for two years. This large mine had been opened in 1867 and did not close until 1988. During its heyday, in the early 1920s, Ashington employed around 4,000 men and boys underground. In 1950, the number working beneath the surface was still over 2,700. The site of this pit is today occupied by Wansbeck Business Park on the northern edge of the town. Several colliery housing rows still survive next to the park.

John remembers the pit being particularly clean and modern. It had roadways with flat roofs. The colliery was a welcome relief from Bates because it was dry. By this time John was married and had a family of his own.

Next John moved to Ellington Colliery, a mine which extended under the sea for several miles. Some of the faces were 10 to 11 kilometres from the shaft bottom. The men rode towards the coal face on trains pulled by small diesel electric engines. Even so, they still had a walk of two or three miles to reach the face after disembarking.

It is clear that John was a good pony handler, because he became a 'special' man at Ellington. This meant he was part of a team of two who could be called upon to do anything from pumping repairs and pipe work to building underground dams or blasting away stone. For all these tasks, a pony was needed to carry equipment and materials.

'Pit ponies never got a true winter coat because they were only occasionally brought to the surface,' says John. 'Their manes and tails were clipped and this made them prickly. All the animals were male, although many years ago mares were used.'

Despite some tales of abuse, the majority of pitmen seem to have treated their ponies with kindness. They would give them titbits and words of encouragement. However, the sturdy little horses were not averse to filching the miners' bait

John Douds collection

Three of the pit ponies at Ellington Colliery. Left to right, Tom, Bass and Toby.

EYE GUARDS FOR PIT PONIES.

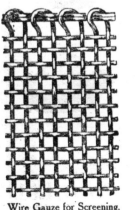

Wire Gauze for Screening.

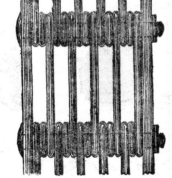

Patent Locket Work for Screening.

Ponies' eyeguards advertised in Reid's Colliery Guide c1920.

(food). They would eat apple cores, orange peel and almost anything else they could find.

John has memories of miners taking their bait to work wrapped in greaseproof paper. After the men had finished their sandwiches the crusts, dirty from their hands, were left. The men would then wrap the grimy crusts in the greaseproof paper, screw it into balls and throw it away. The ponies would seek out the paper balls and unravel them to eat the crusts.

On one occasion, John and another man were with a pony pulling an empty tub. The pony set off at a gallop out of the tail gate and the tub came off the rails. The men and pony fell into 4ft of water. John and his marra picked themselves up, but the unfortunate animal was unable to stand because he was still attached to the derailed tub. The pony was now in danger of drowning. To free him, John would have to remove a bolt which held him to the tub. But the struggling pony had partly raised himself so the bolt was now at an impossible angle. He had no option but to push the pony under the water again for a few brief moments while the bolt was taken out. The animal was then able to get to its feet and recover. All three survived the ordeal.

The largest collieries had several stables, each one covering a different seam or combination of seams. John remembers: 'The stables were immaculate. The animals were well fed and groomed every day.'

He was clearly very fond of the ponies and recalls the names of those he worked with, including Sep, Tom, Bass, Toby and Pike. When Sep retired from Bedlington 'A' he became John's pet and was kept on his allotment together with another pony. During the miners' strike of 1972 he and

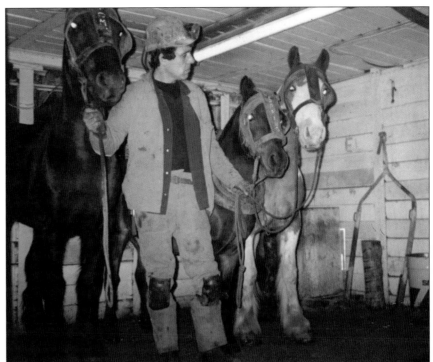

John Douds collection

Miner John Douds with three Ellington Colliery pit ponies. Left to right, Tom, Bass and Toby.

his wife, Carol, were unable to afford the cost of looking after them and they went to a rest home in Carlisle.

John tells of Flax, the last pit pony to work a deep mine in England. He was among the final batch of these hard-working animals to leave Ellington when it closed in 1994. After Flax was brought up in the shaft cage, there were no more left underground. Ellington was closed for only a few months and then reopened, but the ponies never returned. They were the last of the many little pit horses which had served Britain well, as surely as the miners have done.

Last of the pit ponies

The last pit ponies in the North East were retired from Ellington Colliery, Northumberland, in 1994. The last four to be brought up were Carl, Alan, Tom and Flax. Flax was the final one to reach to the surface. These four were also the last ponies to work a deep mine in England. The last of these to die was Carl. He passed away at the National Coal Mining Museum, near Wakefield, West Yorkshire, in 2006. Sparky, another veteran Ellington pony, survived him and, in 2006, was reported to be a remarkable 35 years old. He also lived in retirement at the museum before passing away in 2007.

Another four-legged veteran from Ellington was Pike, who died in 2006. Pike had retired to the Newcastle Dog and Cat Shelter's Benton North Farm, North Tyneside, where his companion was Tony, another pony from the same colliery. Both are believed to have left the mine around 1994. Tony was still living at the Shelter in 2008. Tony and another from Ellington who was reported to be living in stables near Morpeth are among the few pit ponies still surviving in Britain.

The last ponies in the Durham coalfield were the seven which left Sacriston Colliery in 1985. Perhaps the best known of these was Pip, who went to Beamish Museum. However, some of the animals were transferred to Ellington.

John Douds with pit pony Pike at Ellington. After a hard-working life, Pike retired to Newcastle Dog and Cat Shelter's Benton North Farm.

Pike in happy retirement at Newcastle Dog and Cat Shelter, Benton North Farm.

From Pit Lad to Safety Officer

'When you get half way down you think you are coming up.'
Alec Anderson

Among the men who worked at Ellington Colliery was Alec Anderson. Born and brought up in Ashington, he still lives there. Alec spent all his working life in the pits, progressing from pit lad to face worker, from deputy to overman, and then becoming a safety officer. His experience is vast. His father was also a miner as were his grandfather and uncles. 'My father was an old-style hewer and did manual undercutting. One of the collieries where he worked was North Seaton,' says Alec. This pit was close to Ashington, on the northern bank of the River Wansbeck.

Alec remembers the great lockout of 1926 which led to the General Strike in support of the pitmen, who were battling against plans to cut their wages and lengthen their shifts. The miners were reduced to poverty. He recalls going with his father to a colliery waste heap and picking through the stone to try to find coal for their home fire. 'There was no electricity supply to many of the homes. Everything had to be done on the fire, including hot water and cooking, so coal was vital.' The family's only source of lighting was oil lamps or candles.

Soup kitchens were set up during the dispute to share the community's limited food supply among the children. Alec remembers attending one of the soup kitchens at the Hirst Industrial Club in Ashington. Miners brought along their vegetables, and local butchers sometimes gave meat, to supplement the broth that was provided.

Born in 1914, Alec began work at Woodhorn Colliery in 1928. 'I finished school on the Friday and began at the pit on the Monday at 2am. There was no formal training scheme in those days.' On that first shift, Alec descended in the pit cage

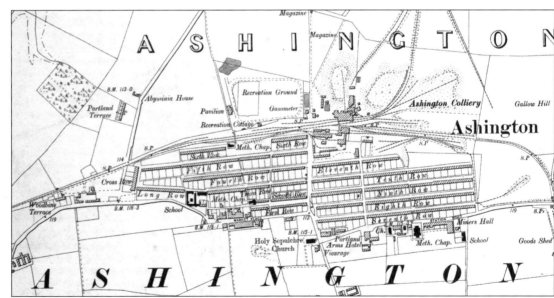

A detail from an Ordnance Survey Map of 1898 shows Ashington Colliery and miners' housing rows. Many such rows still survive in the town, particularly in the Hirst area.

with his father and older brother.

'When you get half way down you think you are coming up,' he declares. It was evidently something of a stomach-turning experience for the new pit lad.

His first job was attaching chains to tubs at the shaft bottom. Alec then gradually progressed through the many skills of mining, including shot-firing and operating coal-cutting machines. The walk to the face might be two or three miles – there were no train rides in this mine in those days. There were no pithead baths at Woodhorn until 1930 so for two years after he began work, Alec, his father and brother had to use a tin bath when they came home. The water was heated on the fire.

Alec points out that miners received a free allowance of coal and Ashington Coal Company houses were rent-free. 'They were the perks of the job.' There were, of course, huge drawbacks too, not least of them the constant risk of death, injury and industrial disease. Alec adds: 'Getting a colliery house was not automatic. You might wait years for one to become available. My father had to wait 20 years.'

He recalls other features typical of the period. Only a few miners at the face had cap lamps in the late 1920s. Many carried glennies. The use of these flame safety lamps was vital. Although this part of Northumberland had not been noted for having gaseous seams, 13 miners died at Woodhorn in 1916 as the result of a firedamp explosion.

Alec went on to become a pit deputy in charge of safety

Ashington Colliery, in the early 1900s.

in one district. Then came promotion to overman, which meant he was in charge of several deputies operating in three or four districts. As an overman he often gave first aid and remembers deaths and injuries. The first time he administered morphine was when a lad aged 15 lost a leg below the knee. The boy had slipped and fallen and a tub had run over his leg, but he recovered and found a job in the colliery offices. According to Alec transport accidents were among the most frequent.

The men operating the coal cutting machines suffered the most exposure to coal dust. In order to keep this terrible hazard in check stone dust, which contained gypsum, was liberally spread about.

Alec also remembers Cavilling Day at Woodhorn. This was the drawing of lots every three months to determine each coalface miner's workplace, known as a cavil or stall. It was an important day, since a poor workplace meant poor pay and more arduous labour. The lots were drawn out of a hat at the colliery offices by officials from the union and the colliery. This lottery was regarded by the pitmen as the only fair way of deciding workplaces and large numbers of men turned out to see if they had been lucky. 'Sometimes you would get a good one and sometimes not.'

Alec served for 34 years at Woodhorn. He too was fond of the ponies and he does not remember them ever being brought to the surface. This seems to have been Ashington Coal Company policy. 'During the annual holiday the ponies were exercised daily by walking them up and down the underground roadways.'

Meanwhile, in 1936 the young pitman had wed. It was a happy and long-lasting marriage. His wife came from a mining family too. This was hardly surprising since thousands of families in South East Northumberland had men working in the area's highly productive mines and Ashington could be described as Northumberland's coal capital. A major feature of the town was row upon row of houses owned by the Ashington Coal Company. They numbered several hundred and many survive in Ashington to this day, particularly in the Hirst area.

After the end of the Second World War, Alec joined a Mines Rescue Service team, based at Ashington, which could be called out in emergencies to pits throughout the North of England. His team went to the Whitehaven disaster of 1947 when 104 men died. He also attended Tyneside's Weetslade explosion scene in 1951. In addition, there were calls to three fires – at Woodhorn, Lynemouth and Dudley. Dudley was the

most serious. 'They had to seal off the pit,' says Alec.

The Mines Rescue Service teams were made up from volunteer pitmen. They carried canaries in cages to act as gas detectors. If there was a lack of oxygen in the air the birds would always be affected, whether the gas encountered was carbon monoxide or blackdamp (chokedamp). Alec explains: 'The canary would flutter about the cage normally, but if gas was present it would sit on its perch and might spread its wings because it had the feeling it was about to fall. The bird might then jump on to the floor of the cage with wings spread.' He adds that the bird was always resuscitated with oxygen after being withdrawn from the gas-hit area. No canary was ever allowed to die. 'We never lost a bird,' he declares. However, having detected gas, the rescue team knew that it was time to put their breathing apparatus on.

A figurine of a miner wearing breathing apparatus was

Tom Yellowley

The end houses of three pit terraces in Ashington – Seventh Row, Eighth Row and Ninth Row – close to the Ashington Colliery. The site of the mine is now occupied by Wansbeck Business Park.

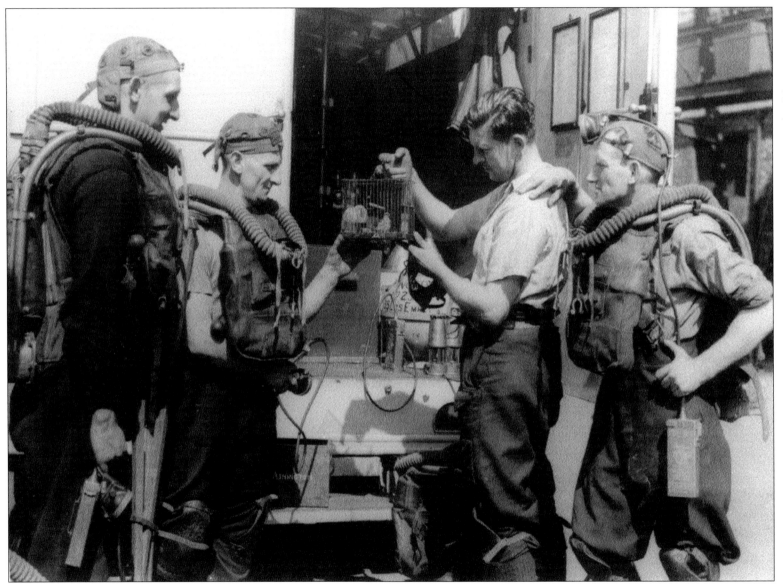

Alec Anderson, second left, with other members of a Mines Rescue Service team at the scene of the Whitehaven Colliery disaster in 1947. They hold a canary for gas detection. A total of 104 men lost their lives in this tragedy.

presented to him, along with a medal, to mark his 15 years in the Mines Rescue Service.

Following his long spell at Woodhorn, Alec became the safety officer at Ellington Colliery. He was in charge of all safety arrangements and walked many miles, checking a host of details for risks and dangers. This pit had diesel electric trains like those at Ashington. Alec often walked the seven miles of track to identify potential hazards and faults. It helped to keep him fit, as did his love of football.

Alec played for a local team, Hirst Corinthians, who were based at the town's Hirst Welfare. The Corinthians were in the Ashington Welfare League, which featured about 20 teams. Legendary Newcastle United footballer Jackie Milburn played in this league at one time. Alec had his moment of glory too. His team won the league championship, the Booth Cup, in the early 1930s. 'The cup was named after the chairman of the Ashington Coal Company.' Alec eventually became a referee.

The veteran miner is proud to have served in the pits. However, mining did take its toll on him. A neck vertebrae problem led to his retirement from Ellington at the age of 61 in 1976. This condition was aggravated by the many knocks his head had taken underground. He had served at this pit for 14 years and was presented with a deputy's safety lamp when he retired.

Alec Anderson is still a remarkably fit man, even though he is in his 90s. His front garden is immaculate, and displays fine hydrangeas. Trains going by on the line behind his home take coal imported from Eastern Europe via the Port of Blyth to the Alcan aluminium smelter at Lynemouth. The black diamonds no longer come from the Ellington pit, which was little over a stone's throw from the smelter. The irony of this is not lost on him.

Tom Yellowley

Veteran miner Alec Anderson who worked at Woodhorn Colliery for 34 years and then became safety officer at Ellington Colliery. He is holding a deputy's safety lamp and the figurine he was presented with to mark his 15 years in the Mines Rescue Service.

Woodhorn Colliery disaster – Unexpected Gas

Tom Yellowley

The Woodhorn Colliery disaster memorial statue. It was formerly sited in Hirst Park, Ashington.

In August 1916, 13 men lost their lives at Woodhorn Colliery as the result of a firedamp explosion in the Main Seam. The blast was believed to have been sparked by a naked light. Inadequate ventilation and failure to check for the presence of gas were also key factors. A ventilation fan was working at a slower speed than usual because several stokers were absent, and an air compressor was off.

Woodhorn had previously been regarded as normally free from methane and the use of naked lights was common, although all deputies were still required to check for gas with their safety lamps before the start of shifts. The miners who died had been working on installing steel girders for roof supports. Eleven of them were married with a total of 34 children between them.

A stone column surmounted by a statue of a miner holding a safety lamp is a memorial to the pitmen who died. It stands on the site of the colliery, which is now the Woodhorn Museum and Archives Centre.

Woodhorn Colliery opened for production in 1898. Many of its buildings and structures have survived, including the two pithead towers with their pairs of winding wheels and the No 1 and No 2 winding engine houses. They are now part of the museum.

The mine operated one of the last working steam winding engines in Britain, until an electric engine was brought from the Fenwick Pit in 1975 and installed in its place in the No 2 house. A huge pit heap once dominated the area behind the colliery, but this was smoothed away to form the Queen Elizabeth II Country Park.

Tom Yellowley

Woodhorn Colliery, Ashington.

Painters from the Mines

The Ashington area produced a group of miners who became nationally acclaimed artists between the two world wars. These talented painters depicted scenes of pit life and the mining communities which they knew intimately. Their subjects included whippet racing, pigeon crees and the chippy, as well as underground scenes. They had been encouraged by Robert Lyon, a Newcastle art lecturer from the Workers' Educational Association.

The painters, known as the Ashington Group, included Oliver Kilbourn, Fred Laidler, Jimmy Floyd, George Blessed, Harry Wilson and many others. Most, but not all, were miners. The group's first exhibition was at the Hatton Gallery, Newcastle, in 1936. Over 40 years later, in 1980, group paintings were exhibited in Beijing at the invitation of the Chinese government. Today, a collection of their paintings is on display in the East Gallery at the Woodhorn museum and archives centre.

Whippets, by George Blessed, 1939.

County Durham too has produced its share of fine pitmen artists. The Spennymoor Settlement was set up in 1931 to help ordinary people of the area develop their cultural talents and skills. This centre of the arts, crafts and drama had a sketching club which included among its members the highly talented artists Norman Cornish and Tom McGuinness, both miners. Their works are widely acknowledged as superb.

One of Norman Cornish's best known works is his impressive mural on the theme of the Durham Gala, which can be found at County Hall, Durham. Norman, from the Spennymoor area, worked for many years at Dean & Chapter Colliery, Ferryhill.

Tom McGuinness's work has also won great acclaim. His best-known pictures include *Early Morning Shift*, *Harvey Manrider*, *Tailgate*, and *The Pit Road*. Tom was a Bevin Boy from the Bishop Auckland area but worked in the pits for many years after the Second World War, serving at Fishburn and East Hetton (Kelloe) collieries. He passed away in 2006.

The Ashington Group, 1938, photographed by Julian Trevelyan.

Pithead Baths and Welfare Schemes

Although there is a report of the owners of Cramlington Colliery providing miners with baths at the pithead as early as 1855, this was an exceptional case. Not until the 20th century did a real movement get underway towards providing these facilities generally in the Great Northern Coalfield. The first 'modern' pithead baths in Northumberland were opened at Ellington Colliery in March 1924 and the first in County Durham at Boldon Colliery in February 1927. It took many years for most of the region's pits to be equipped with these shower facilities, which were a great leap forward for the miners' quality of life. The pitman was no longer forced to return home covered in black dust and grime and his wife was saved the daily chore of filling and emptying a tin bath.

At the trail-blazing Ellington, the Miners' Welfare Fund provided the cash to build the baths and men contributed money from their wages to help pay for maintenance and running costs. The employers also contributed towards these costs. This set a pattern for the future

Some collieries did not have pithead baths until well after the Second World War. One example was Whittle drift mine in Northumberland, where there were no baths until 1967. Winston Pile, of Morpeth, worked at Whittle and remembers catching the bus home covered in pit dust during the late 1950s and early 60s.

The 1920 Mining Act established the national Miners' Welfare Fund, a recommendation of the Sankey Commission. Colliery owners contributed a levy of one penny per ton of coal produced towards this fund, which financed schemes to improve the life of the pitman and his family. From 1926, a levy was also placed on coal royalties. This extra funding gave an impetus to the construction of more pithead baths.

A Miners' Welfare Commission was established to administer the fund and money was allocated to each coalfield area to help provide welfare halls, sports fields, children's playgrounds, pithead baths, canteens and other facilities such as libraries. Welfare halls (generally known simply as 'the welfare' or 'the institute') were among the most important schemes to result from this initiative. They became social centres for many events, including dances and wedding celebrations.

Tom Yellowley

Deserted. Miners' clothing lockers at the disused Lynemouth Colliery baths.

Donkey Stone and Dadding

'The dess bed, the feather bed, the best bed of all. Shake it up and shake it up and dad it against the wall.'
(North East children's rhyme)

The miners could not have done their job without the support of the women in their families. Jean Harrison was born in Pegswood and went to the village schools. Her father, Willie 'Jumper' Watson worked at Pegswood Colliery. She and her brother and sisters all helped to clean his clothes and equipment after he finished shifts. They gave his helmet, kneepads and boots a good polishing.

Jean remembers cleaning the grooves in the soles of her father's boots with a knife. His trousers were hit ('dadded') against the back wall to remove the dust and hung on a clothes horse to dry out – conditions in the mine could be wet.

Water was heated on the range (in later years in an electric boiler that the washing was boiled in) to fill the tin bath for her father coming home. When her father was on the fore shift, which started at 2am, her mother did not go to bed. She slept in a chair near the fire until the knocker came at 1am.

Jean's mother would then wake her husband and prepare his bait tin and carbide lamp. The bait was always jam sandwiches. She remembers her father testing his carbide lamp with a flint and spitting in it. The spitting was a mystery to her – she never found out why he did this.

Jean's mother never seemed to stop working. She baked bread twice a week, including stotties and square loaves in tins. Miners' wives in the region had a tradition of keeping their homes particularly clean and neat and Jean's mother

The interior of a pitman's cottage at Marley Hill, c1900.

was no exception. The saying was that 'more people pass the house than come in', so the outside had to be as clean as the inside and the front step was cleaned with a 'donkey' stone. (Donkey stone was a chalk-like powdered stone mixed with bleach and water and set into a mould, often carrying a stamped donkey emblem). All the work had to be finished by Saturday.

On Sundays the routine was a little different. The meat for dinner would have been cooked on Saturday evening and if they were lucky they could have a chunk of home made bread dipped in the meat juices for supper. Her mother baked on Sunday morning, making apple pie, date pie (made from a block of stoned dates), egg custard and scones. Her father liked his scones a day old, so he ate his on the Monday. In the afternoon, Jean's mother would lie and rest in the front room. Left-over meat and vegetables from dinner were fried to make pan haggerty for tea. Jean cannot remember her mother ever going out, apart from to the shops.

As children, she and her sisters and brother took the vegetable peelings to the neighbour's pigs and they sometimes received bacon or black or white pudding in return. However, the pigs would not get the apple peelings; she and her brother and sisters would fight over those.

Betty McLaren, of South Shields, is also the daughter of a miner. Her father, John Sinclair, known as Little Jackie, worked at St Hilda Colliery in the town. His family originated from the Shetlands and were crofters. She writes: 'He had many skills but, because of a spinal defect, he was only 4ft 11in, and he could not get other work except in the mines where his height was an asset.' Betty can remember her father coming home from work with 'a Technicolor face'. His hair, eyebrows and eyelashes were black with coal dust clinging to them, his eye rims and lips red and 'his brown (hazel) eyes and his white teeth showed through his smile'.

Her mother always had a large pan and a black kettle of hot water on the fire bars and hob ready for her father's bath. The oval-shaped tin bath was about 3ft wide by 3ft long. 'Although we lived in a two-roomed flat, I never witnessed him bathing'.

Betty and her brothers were given the job of 'dadding' her father's pit clothes against the backyard wall to get the coal dust out before they could be washed.

Betty McLaren, the daughter of a miner who worked at St Hilda Colliery, South Shields.

This was a common chore for the children of pitmen. Betty remembers a party game that was played while a little song was sung. They stood in a circle and one person went round the ring, carrying a cushion, while everyone sang: 'The dess bed, the feather bed, the best bed of all. Shake it up and shake it up and dad it against the wall'. A dess bed was one that could be folded and stored away. This saved space in small colliery homes. Betty continues: 'It was great when the pit baths were installed and he came home clean'.

After the 1926 stoppage, unemployment hit the coalfield in a big way. Her father was paid off in 1928 and did not work again until 1936. 'I suppose it was probably a reprisal from the bosses for the men having gone on strike in the first place'. The years he was out of work were hard, although he made some money sign painting and helping the local coalman to look after his horses.

During this time of unemployment for pitmen Betty says 'there was a lot of unrest amongst the miners and the government and it encouraged miners to turn further to the left and embrace Communism'. Her father's friend would come to the back door with the *Daily Worker* and *Russia Today*. Her mother was terrified that they would be sent to jail. 'My father was probably just buying the papers because his friend would get commission and it would help to feed his large family.'

When John Sinclair returned to work it was at Harton Colliery, also in South Shields. 'He sometimes worked in seams that were only 14ins to 16ins high and they were lying on their bellies in 4-6 inches of water, absolutely soaking and cutting stone to find coal (he was a stoneman) and this is where his small stature came in useful'. She adds: 'Needless to say there were often falls of coal covering the men over. Some were killed'.

Betty had wondered why her father only took bread and sugar for his bait. He would never eat sweets or puddings at home. He told her that if he got 'happed owaa' or 'buried in' that the margarine and sugar made a syrupy combination that would 'quench a thirst for a while'.

It seemed that every day her father came home with a cut or bruise. On one occasion a manager noticed a cut on his face. 'The first cut was on his chin, the next week it was on his nose and the third week it was on his brow and the

Betty McLaren's father, pitman John Sinclair ('Little Jackie'), right, with his bowls trophies.

manager said to him 'Hi Jack, where's that cut gannin next?'

The worst cut he got was about seven inches long on his back, across his shoulder blades. 'My mother bathed it and bathed it till she nearly fainted. It was open nearly half an inch and she was trying to get as much of the coal dust out as she could. But as we all know it was impossible to get out and it healed as a navy blue stripe forever.'

The family lived about 20 minutes' walk from Harton Colliery and once they had the opportunity to move closer to the pithead. Her father would not consider it. 'He said after being underground as many hours, he needed the walk in the fresh air to clear his lungs of the coal dust and he declared that without the walk he would die'.

He sometimes visited the Perseverance Club, Hudson Street, near Tyne Dock Station. It was frequented by miners and local politicians of the day. 'They used to meet and argue politics for hours, much to my mother's dismay.'

Betty's father died just before the end of the Second World War at the age of 54. 'He was a very popular man and everyone liked him. There is something special about miners, it's their friendship and love.'

Madge Davies was born in a pitman's cottage, the Old Row, High Spen, in 1926, the year of the 'Big Strike'. Her father, Halford 'Albert' Harwood, worked as a hewer at High Spen Pit and a drift mine close by. Her mother's brother, Hal Smith, worked there too. She writes: 'They were respectable miners, good at their jobs. They worked in water and dust, with only spades and pickaxes, in their pit vests and hoggers [shorts, though originally used to describe the stockings worn with shorts].' The villages around High Spen, such as Highfield and Chopwell, supplied the manpower for the pits, although the 'working conditions in the Durham pits in the 1920s and 30s were very poor and lots of men had accidents'.

Madge pays tribute to miners' wives who 'stood by their men and made their homes clean and cosy with plenty of hot water in the fire boiler so they could have a bath in front of the fire in the old tin bath'. During the strike the men hunted rabbits and sold them to the local butcher for threepence. The women would 'make broth from vegetables and leeks grown in the gardens or allotments'. She also remembers the stone floors of the houses and cottages being kept warm with hand-made rugs (clippy mats) made by the wives in the evenings when the children were in bed.

Old pit cottages at Marley Hill, a Durham mining village not far from High Spen, c1900.

Many pitmen loved to get out in the open air to grow vegetables or flowers. Madge remembers rows of dog daisies and marigolds in the front gardens. The men often kept canaries in cages in the home or bred them for shows, keeping them in a hut built on the allotment or at the end of the garden. Madge's father was involved in 'boxing and football teams [Spen Black and White] as the miners all loved getting plenty of exercise in the fresh air'.

When work was plentiful her father saved his pocket money to take the family on two weeks' holiday. They went to Cullercoats, Whitley Bay or South Shields. Her father said it was 'to get away from the smell of dust from the pitheaps' which surrounded High Spen village. They stayed at Cullercoats for bed and breakfast. Most of the houses were occupied by fishermen. It would cost £1.10s (£1.50) for a week. 'We all slept in one room and washed in the kitchen but it was a happy time and everyone was friendly.'

Gateshead Libraries & Arts

Members of the Spen Black and White football team, c1900. Madge Davies' father, Halford Harwood, played for the club. He was a hewer at High Spen pit.

She also remembers going on Sunday School trips to the coast. 'We would go in coaches owned by Robsons, and all be given a tambourine. We looked like a snake as we trailed down the roads in a line and when we passed through the villages we all banged our tambourines.'

Madge's father suffered from bronchitis and also contracted pleurisy linked to working in wet seams. He left the pits just after the Second World War to run a fruit and vegetable shop in Lemington.

Margaret Cockburn was brought up in Whitley Bay but her father George (Sam) Haigh was born at Coxhoe, County Durham, in 1914. He started in the pits at the age of 14, although Margaret does not know much about his early years in mining. He thought there was no future for him in the pits and joined the Army as a regular soldier. She remembers a tattoo on her father's arm. 'It was a pit lamp with the words Never Again'. He was stationed at Tynemouth Castle where he met Margaret's mother who lived in the village.

After the Second World War the only work Margaret's father could get was back in the pits. He started at the Rising Sun. They lived in Whitley Bay and he travelled to the pit by moped along the New Coast Road to work the midnight-8am night shift as a coal cutter. 'He would take a fruited tea cake and jam every single shift.'

Her mother worried if he was late home. 'It would usually mean he had been in an accident, often from falls. He once almost severed two fingers which were stitched but never really worked again'. He suffered from a bad back which could be so painful he would cry out when getting up from a chair. 'He had to take painkillers to do his night shift'. Margaret also remembers her father 'coughing and spitting constantly'.

The miners were issued with halibut oil capsules in the winter and he would bring home coal tar soap, 'pit soap', which 'lasted for ages'.

While at the Rising Sun, Margaret's family attended sports days at the mine's playing fields. Margaret entered every race.

When the pit closed her father took redundancy. He did not work for about two years. 'He didn't know what to do with himself and took a job at Eccles.' He stayed until this mine also closed.

Dorothy Pattinson, of Crawcrook, is the daughter of George Shotton, a hewer who worked all his life – except for a spell of service in the Army – at Greenside Colliery. He walked around one and a half miles to the pit to begin his shift. Dorothy still remembers him coming home completely blackened by a night shift at the coalface. George's brother, Tommy, was also a hewer at Greenside and they joined the Army together during the First World War. Tall – both were over 6ft – serving in the Coldstream Guards.

The pitman's daughter was brought up in a colliery-owned terraced house in Crawcrook – she still lives in one, just across the road from her childhood home. Her father paid rent for the family house to the Stella Coal Company and, like most miners' families, they received a free coal allowance.

Dorothy Pattinson, of Crawcrook. Her father, George Shotton, was a hewer at Greenside Colliery.

Dorothy recalls that her father generally worked the midnight-8am shift. He carried his bait in a tin box – it was always jam sandwiches. He also took a tin bottle of water with him.

'When he got home he was black and very tired. He wouldn't take a bath until after he had his breakfast, he was so hungry.' He liked kippers and would eat them with his coal dust-covered fingers, washed down with a pot (mug) of tea. Dorothy hated washing up the blackened pot. He then lay down in front of the fire, exhausted. Gradually, he would recover and then take his bath. George always told his wife not to wash his back 'too much as it will weaken it'. This was a common belief among pitmen throughout the North East.

Built in the early 1900s, the family house had a small bathroom area, separated from the kitchen by a curtain, so George did not have to use a tin bath like large numbers of miners in the region. Their home also had a traditional-style fire range and an outside lavatory. Luckily, they had a garden, rather than a yard, and George had 'green fingers'. He grew vegetables for the family and kept hens.

Before they moved into the colliery house, the family lived for a while in a hut. There were others living in huts too. 'One of the families was so poor, they took the hookey mats from the floor and put them on their beds as blankets.'

Daughters as well as wives had plenty to keep them occupied. Dorothy remembers using donkey stone to whiten the step at the front door, blackening the fire grate, 'dadding' her father's work clothes and cleaning his boots with a knife. The clothes would be put to dry next to the fireside, ready for the next shift.

On one occasion, her father received a bad cut underneath his eye during his work. Her mother bathed it, but it was impossible to get all the dust out. He bore the scar for the rest of his life.

Dorothy remembers hearing the local colliery band in the morning as they marched through the streets of the village before setting off by bus for the Durham Miners' Gala. 'My father never missed the Big Meeting.'

One day Dorothy heard an alarm at the colliery. 'I heard the siren. My mother said something must have happened.' Her father had been on night shift as usual and was asleep. They decided to wake him up. George 'had to go', and set off for the pit. Three men had been killed.

Dorothy's brother-in-law, John Parker, is the son of a miner who worked at Clara Vale Colliery, close to Crawcrook. As a boy he was taken down the Emma Pit on a school visit. Conditions seemed primitive. 'The men were crawling on their bellies to mine the coal.' John adds: 'What struck me was the comradeship between them. They looked after each other.'

George died at the age of 81 in 1977 from pneumoconiosis – the miner's disease. This condition causes serious breathing problems. As a face worker he was particularly exposed to the dust. 'They were in the front line,' says John.

Dorothy Pattinson collection

Two hewers. Dorothy Pattinson's father George Shotton (seated) with his brother Tommy during their service in the Coldstream Guards.

Growing up in a pit village

Industrial archaeologist Dr Stafford M. Linsley grew up in the mining village of Boldon Colliery where his father was a deputy at the pit. He writes of his boyhood: 'Pit heaps were our adventure playground, and coal-fired kitchen ranges our delight, except when we had to get the coal in, or take ash out. But it was well worth doing such chores if some of grandma's stotty cake, still warm, and with treacle on it was the reward.

Boldon Colliery c1920.

'Noises of various sorts characterised the village. The knocker-up rattling windows with his long pole, the incessant drone of the mine ventilation fan, the buzzers and hooters and bells associated with the surface workings of the mines, the whirring of the pulley wheels as men or materials were being wound in the shaft, and of course the coal waggons being marshalled before being taken down the former Stanhope & Tyne Railway which bisected the village. And the melodic sounds of chapel choirs, or the colliery brass band for which my dad wrote some tunes, but equally as evocative for me, Uncle Alf singing like Joseph Lock while my dad played the piano.

'The Miners' Institute had an excellent library, but more importantly, four full-sized billiard tables where I learned at a fairly early age the rudiments of the green baize arts, including gambling games which utilised small skittles.

'But there was a down-side as well. Dad's splitting headaches after a day's inhalation of powder reek while shot-firing, Uncle Alf dragging himself to the pit while he was dying, my nightmares after the Easington Colliery disaster of 1951, and the regular sight of ex-miners shuffling along the streets, a few paces at a time, pausing to catch breath while coughing up black spit.'

Ex-colliery houses form a long row in North Road, Boldon Colliery. The entrance to the mine was only yards away.

Dr Linsley comes from a family of at least three generations of miners. His great grandfather, Thomas Linsley senior, was an Independent Methodist preacher. In 1885, at the age of 31, he was killed by a fall of stone while working at Monkwearmouth Colliery.

Hoggers and Mufflers

A hewer from C.H. Steavenson's 'Colliery Workmen, Sketched at Work', 1912. Artist Steavenson was manager of Redheugh Colliery.

Of the clothing worn by North East pitmen, industrial archaeologist Dr Stafford Linsley writes: 'The varied working environments, both above and underground, were not generally conducive to uniformity. For example, an onsetter working at the foot of a downcast shaft might need protection against the cold air, while a shaft-bottom worker at an upcast shaft, where the air was often humid, might wear few clothes. Indeed, until well past the middle of the 20th century, face workers frequently removed most, and sometimes all of their clothes, on reaching their place of work; it was said of Shilbottle Colliery, in 1842, that "the men work completely naked".'

Dr Linsley quotes John Leifchild's description of hewers' working attire in 1856: 'Their pit dress is made entirely of coarse flannel, and consists of a long jacket with large side-pockets, a waistcoat, a flannel shirt, a pair of short drawers, and a pair of stout trousers worn over them. Add to these a pair of 'hoggers', or footless worsted stockings, a tight-fitting round leather cap, and you have the hewer ready for the pit.'

Woodhorn Colliery pitman Alec Anderson says that canvas caps were commonly worn in the 1920s and 1930s, with deputies and overmen wearing leather ones. Those not working at the face might wear flat caps. Hard hats were not widely introduced until after the Second World War.

Wearside miner Jim Wilson remembers the men wore mufflers round their necks going outbye. Mufflers were also worn going inbye, but taken off if the men reached a warm working area: 'The ordinary miner wore warm, stout clothing. When he was working on the face he would wear a minimum of clothing, normally vest, shorts, stockings and, at some mines, stockings with the feet cut off to roll over the top of his boots to stop the small coals getting down into his boots, and knee pads.'

He adds: 'When I first started work in the Sixties the colliery overmen wore knee length trousers tucked into the tops of their stockings and also carried a yardstick. This was their badge of rank and it also could be looked upon as a status symbol differentiating them from the rest of us. They along with the deputies also wore waistcoats. Fitters and electricians wore overalls, whereas we must have seemed like their poorer cousins wearing hand-me-downs. All this changed in the late Seventies when the workwear scheme was introduced. We all looked alike in our orange overalls … Protective clothing was introduced some time in the Eighties. This was due to the changes in health and safety rules. All of a sudden the extra equipment we had was ear muffs, goggles, gloves, reflective jackets. While all this gear was a nuisance to carry, it could only have been for the better.'

Homes for retired miners and their wives

Housing built by the Durham Aged Mineworkers' Homes Association can be found throughout much of County Durham and parts of Tyne and Wear. Today, the association provides more than 1,600 homes, mainly for retired people, and preference is still given to ex-miners.

The association points out that the foundation of this philanthropic organisation was the result of the vision of Joseph Hopper, a miner from Gateshead and Methodist lay preacher, who believed that a man who had served in the coal mines from the age of 12 to 65 or beyond deserved better than to be evicted from his tied colliery house when he retired without the prospect of a decent alternative home. Such accommodation was vitally needed for elderly pitmen and their wives.

The way forward was shown by miners of the union lodge at Boldon Colliery who opened Down Hill House at West Boldon, a converted mansion, as accommodation for retired pitmen in c1897.

Durham Aged Mineworkers' Homes Association

The first batch of homes provided by Durham Aged Mineworkers' Homes Association are opened at Haswell Moor in 1899. They were known collectively as the John Johnson Memorial Home.

The Durham Aged Mineworkers' Homes Association was formed in 1896-98 under the leadership of Joseph Hopper, who became its secretary, and supported by miners' MP John Wilson, Durham Miners' Association financial secretary John Johnson and the Bishop of Durham, Brooke Foss Westcott.

Its earliest homes were existing properties no longer required for working miners. The first group to be opened were at Haswell Moor, in 1899, where the association had purchased the complete village for housing following closure of the pit. Similar schemes involving existing houses followed at Shincliffe, Shotton Colliery and Houghall.

The initiative gained momentum. In the early 1900s, houses were built in almost every union lodge area in County Durham and according to the association by the outbreak of the First World War in 1914 a total of 475 homes had been constructed and a number of single men's hostels provided. Among the first purpose-built properties were 12 cottages completed in the Wrekenton-Springwell area in 1904. The little settlement was known as 'Wallace Village'.

The Durham miners' union lodges were key backers of the housing movement, the men contributing money from their pay. The homes are featured on many lodge banners. The association says: 'A small weekly levy voluntarily donated from the miners' wages plus donations of land and materials from mine owners and others, allowed the homes to be constructed and let free of charge.'

The 1920s saw many homes built, with between 50 and 100 completed annually. The Durham Aged Mineworkers' Homes Association declares: 'Although the Durham coalfield is no more, the association has survived and prospered, and continues to provide good quality homes for older people, the less physically active or disabled.'

In 1900, an association was also formed to provide homes for elderly Northumberland miners and their wives. The Northumberland Aged Mineworkers' Homes Association opened its first row of cottages at East Chevington in 1902, a village which eventually disappeared with the closure of its drift mine. Members of the county's union paid a levy from their wages to help fund the building of homes. Today, the organisation provides 540 homes for former miners, their wives or widows.

As well as aged miners' homes another feature of pit communities has been the numerous Methodist chapels. These chapels – Primitive, Wesleyan or Independent – are to be found throughout the coalfield. In the 19th and early 20th centuries active mining trade unionists were frequently Primitive Methodists, a denomination also known as 'the Ranters'. The other Methodists were also represented in their ranks. Tommy Hepburn, William Crawford, John Wilson, Peter Lee and Northumberland Miners' leader William Straker were all Methodists.

The New Hartley Memorial Cottages, completed by the Northumberland Aged Mineworkers' Homes Association in 1910 at New Hartley. They commemorate the 204 men and boys who died in the North East's worst pit disaster.

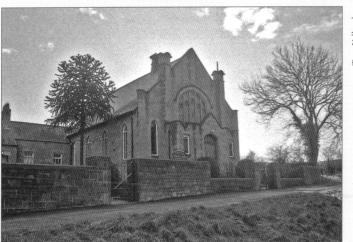

A Methodist chapel at Clara Vale.

Marras Beneath the Surface

'The imprint of my figure was left on the sheet.'
Eddie Job

There are few towns or villages in the North East where former miners cannot be found. The deep pits have vanished but the pitmen are still there, hidden not too far beneath the surface of the region's communities. They are a gradually diminishing army of marras, comrades in the unceasing war they waged against the dangers underground, and they have not forgotten their strong friendships, their shared hardships and their mines.

One example is Robert Bourne, of Blackfell, Washington, who began work at Usworth Colliery, Washington, in 1929 at the age of 14. Some of the districts in this mine had very low passages and in the wettest seams there was a foot of water in places. Robert worked as a putter and pony driver. 'I could handle the ponies fine,' he says. With his pony, he would take the loaded tubs to the landings. He thought the hewer's job was tougher than a putter's because of the dust they encountered at the coalface: 'Terrible.'

Several men were killed during Robert's time at Usworth, including an overman. One lad died when his coat was caught in the cog of a rope haulage machine.

After two years at Usworth, Robert transferred to Washington F Pit, the oldest mine in the area. It dated back to the 18th century. At this colliery, Robert carried out repair work to roof supports, again working with ponies and carrying girders inbye. However, in 1941 he left Washington F to serve in the RAF.

After the Second World War, Robert eventually went back

Veteran miner Robert Bourne with his grandson, Andrew Glendinning. Washington F Pit is in the background.

to mining, this time at Washington Glebe Pit. He helped to train mining apprentices in transport at the shaft bottom, working as part of the onsetter's team. He retired from the Glebe when it closed.

Robert, like so many North East pitmen, comes from a mining family. His grandfather was a hewer at Washington F and his father was a colliery blacksmith.

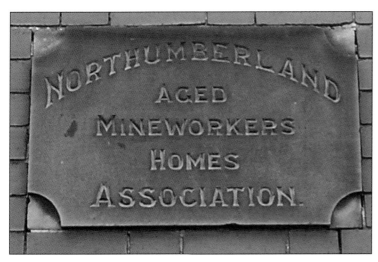

Richard Smith

A stone plaque on the row of cottages at Longbenton.

Richard Smith

Eddie Job, of Longbenton, was from a mining family. Both his father and grandfather were pitmen. 'My father died from pneumoconiosis – he was a driller for shot-firing and this exposed him to a lot of dust.'

Eddie, who passed away in November 2007, lived with his wife Tina in a row of 10 cottages built by the Northumberland Aged Mine Workers' Homes Association in 1913-14. All the houses are occupied by former pitmen and their wives or widows.

The people in the row are great friends. During the summer, the retired miners often sit beside the back lane behind Eddie's yard, known by the neighbours as Canny Crack Corner, recounting tales and enjoying a sing-song.

Eddie worked at the Rising Sun Colliery, Wallsend, for 30 years, starting as a lad at the age of 14 during the Second World War. He remembered a German air raid on the shipyards. He and his marras were ascending in the pit cage when it was stopped in the shaft because of the bombing.

Former Rising Sun miner Eddie Job and his wife, Tina, outside their Longbenton cottage, built by the Northumberland Aged Mineworkers' Homes Association in 1913-14.
Eddie passed away in November 2007.

The winding engine was put on standstill and they were stuck in the cage for two hours. The miners could hear the bombs but not the aircraft.

Eddie suffered a broken arm in a tub accident underground at the age of 15. After another injury he arrived at Newcastle General Hospital but was reluctant to lie on a white-sheeted bed as he was covered in black dust and grime from the pit. The doctor assured him that he was perfectly entitled to lie on the sheet as the miners contributed money from their wages towards the hospital. Eventually Eddie did lie down and remembered: 'The imprint of my figure was left on the sheet.'

On one shift the roof collapsed with a 'thunderous' noise. The wooden supports gave way and crashed down on a pony and tub. His workmate suggested that unmarried Eddie should be the one to free the animal! But in the end it was a deputy who intervened and released the pony.

Although he worked on the north side of the Tyne, Eddie often went to the Durham Miners' Gala. He would meet up with friends from Doncaster on the Gala field. He never forgot the sight of the Easington Lodge banner draped in black crepe following the disaster of 1951.

The mining tradition continued in Eddie's family when his son, also named Eddie, joined his father at the colliery. With the closure of the Rising Sun in 1969, Eddie junior

Tom Yellowley

Washington F Pit's Victorian winding engine house and headgear. The pit opened in 1777 and closed in 1968. It is now managed by Tyne & Wear Museums for Sunderland City Council. The winding engine can still be seen working.

moved to the Nottinghamshire coalfield.

Frank Keerie, of Hebburn, trained at Washington F Pit as an electrician and worked there for seven years. Born in Washington Village, he started at the mine at the age of 14 during the Second World War. The pit heap at Washington F towered over the row of colliery houses where his family lived. Frank's father was a miner, but Frank's mother did not seem to want her son to join him at work.

Frank remembers an accident when a stone weighing

perhaps a ton came down on a friend. The miner suffered serious injuries and although he eventually returned to underground work, it was not long before he was hit by 'blackouts' and had to give up the job.

Brian Welsh, of Coxlodge, Newcastle, was a miner for 31 years. Starting at Hazlerigg Colliery, near Wideopen, in 1954 at the age of 15, one of his first jobs was carrying shot-firing powder in large tin caddies. He and his workmates took the powder from the magazine to the lamp cabin area to be picked up by the men as they came on shift. They were known as powder monkeys.

At 16, Brian began work underground as a pony putter, handling the empty tubs. In those days, there were around 70 ponies and three stables at Hazlerigg. He is full of praise for these little horses and would keep one as a pet if he could. Later, Brian progressed to face work – filling the coal on to the conveyers and operating cutter machines. During this period he suffered a broken wrist in an accident involving a pony.

Brian did a spell at Burradon Colliery, training in the use of power loading with shearers. Production ceased at Hazlerigg in 1961 and Brian and a considerable number of his fellow pitmen transferred to nearby Weetslade Colliery.

After Weetslade, came a move to Brenkley, an extension of the old Seaton Burn Pit workings. Brenkley was a drift mine. It was here that Brian had a serious accident while on a coal cutting shift. Two of his vertebrae were broken when a 10-yard wedge of stone collapsed, clipping his back. He was taken to Newcastle General Hospital and was off work for 11 months. However, he did eventually manage to return to face working at Brenkley, progressing to shearer power loading. Brian left mining in January 1986 when Brenkley closed.

Keeping racing pigeons meant that Brian made friends

Tom Yellowley collection

Above: A postcard view of Seaton Burn Colliery, early 1900s.

Below: Brenkley Drift mine was situated about a mile to the west of Seaton Burn Colliery. This picture shows the old trackway for the wire-rope haulage railway which took the coal from Brenkley to Seaton Burn Colliery. It was then transported onwards through the mineral rail system of the area.

Tom Yellowley

with miners from Blackhall in County Durham. They were a huge support to Brian and his family during the 1984-85 miners' strike as they delivered food at his house during that difficult time.

As a face worker, Brian was exposed to large amounts of dust and today, like so many pitmen, he suffers from shortness of breath.

Winston Pile, of Morpeth went to Ashington Mining School at the age of 15, and then joined the workforce at Whittle Colliery, a drift mine, not far from the Shilbottle pit. The men rode below in electric cars.

Winston has done every job down the pit, except being a gaffer such as a deputy or overman. While working as a filler he would sometimes lie on his side shovelling coal for seven hours with water coming from the roof 'like it was raining'. He worked in cramped areas where the spaces between the roof and floor were under 3ft, and on some occasions under 2ft. When a massive section of stone fell from the roof a man was killed. Winston was working on the same face at the same time and realised it could have been him or any one of his workmates.

Early in 2008 it was reported that three companies had expressed an interest in the possibility of re-opening Whittle Colliery. The site was up for auction.

Patrick Gilbert, of Newcastle, spent five years in mining and remembers many of the details with great clarity, even though his last job down a pit was in the late 1950s. He started work at Backworth Colliery in 1949 at the age of 15. This mine featured two pits, the Maud and the Eccles, which were only about 100 yards apart. However, they were largely separated by a geological fault.

Patrick's first jobs were in the pit prop yard and on the screens. After a six-week training course at Weetslade

Colliery, at 16 he began work at the shaft bottom of the Maud. This was 1,100ft below the surface. His job was to catch the empty tubs as they came down a slope from the cage area and clip them together for their journey inbye. This was heavy work.

Later came a spell operating the tub system in the Yard Seam, which produced quality household coal. He then moved on to the Bensham Seam, which had a tub system operating on a 1 in 4 slope with continuous wire rope haulage. Here he had a downward-sloping walk of about a mile, bent almost double, to reach his work area.

Patrick remembers that in the early 1950s an ascending cage containing full tubs suddenly crashed down the Maud shaft, causing considerable damage. Luckily, the men at the bottom heard it coming and ran from the area so there were no injuries or deaths.

At the pithead baths the water was always hot and men coming off shift would run to them to make sure they were out in time to catch the bus. Missing it would mean a wait of half an hour. The colliery ran a store which sold hats, boots and other items, engineering and fabrication shops, a facility for sharpening coal cutter machine picks, a sawmill, stores for equipment and oils, a first aid station and a canteen.

After National Service in the Army and a spell doing other jobs, Patrick returned to the Maud, but it was not long before he got a transfer to Westoe Colliery at South Shields.

Alan Green, of Dudley, is the son of a miner. His father, Ernest, was a hewer at Harraton Colliery, near Washington, where he worked all his life. Alan's brother, John, worked as a putter at this mine, and at other collieries. The family lived at Barley Mow, between Birtley and Chester-le-Street. Alan remembers walking to the pit with his mother on pay day so that she could collect his father's earnings. His father usually

Backworth Colliery, c. early 1900s. The colliery featured two pits, the Maud and the Eccles, largely separated by a geological fault.

walked the three miles to the pit. His bait was always jam sandwiches. Pitmen often preferred this high energy food, because it was light and not too filling so they did not feel uncomfortable in confined spaces.

Harraton Colliery was known as 'Nova Scotia', or simply 'Coatia' to the men – in the early days of the pit many Scots came to work there and a nearby settlement was named Nova Scotia. Alan treasures the 'Pioneer's Diploma' which was presented to Ernest to mark his 50 years' membership of the Durham Miners' Association. As a strong trade unionist, Ernest never missed the Durham Miners' Gala.

Ernest lost a toe as a result of an accident in the pit. 'I knew he had been injured, but was not told the details.' Alan remembers a teenage boy being killed at Harraton. The pit closed for that day, as a mark of respect.

Leek Shows and Pigeon Racing, by Tony Henderson

The great traditional North East pursuits of prize leek growing and pigeon racing have their roots deep in mining culture. After long days spent working underground, and the industrial grime of the colliery, mineworkers craved fresh air, contact with the natural world and a creative way to spend their leisure time which contrasted with the harsh realities of the pit. The garden, or allotment, provided an inexpensive answer. There was also a practical side. Growing vegetables, keeping hens and in earlier days pigs, was a valuable contribution to the family economy. Providing fresh produce was also important in that it meant families were not utterly dependent on the colliery.

Tom Yellowley

Allotments at High Handenhold, near Beamish. The Handenhold Pit was part of West Pelton Colliery. Vegetables grown on the miners' allotments or gardens would help to feed their families, and were particularly important during long strikes and lockouts.

Growing flowers such as the stalwarts of the allotment, dahlias and chrysanthemums, gave pitmen the opportunity to enjoy the beauty of their blooms, away from the utilitarian grind of work. It also allowed pitmen to escape at least temporarily into their own world, away from the demands of work and family responsibilities.

The tight sense of community in pit settlements fostered a sense of competition, and the leek show and pigeon race were perfect stages. The aim of the leek grower has always been to nurture specimens which combine size with quality – the sheen of the white barrel, the spotless, combed roots, the lustrous green flags, or leaves with stands of two or three leeks as uniformly alike as possible. Years of cross-breeding have developed improved and winning strains which would be eagerly sought-after by growers. After many months of skillful devotion to the leeks, the day of the show was a heady mix of anticipation, subdued excitement and the earthy, leafy smell of serried ranks of benched exhibits. Early shows offered household goods as prizes, later these were replaced by cash prizes. But it was never just about the money. A winning stand brought respect, status and kudos in a community which knew how much skill and application was needed to take the top spots.

The same striving for perfection and the keen edge of competition underpins pigeon rearing and racing. The brightly painted crees have long been a feature of the coalfield landscape. The only listed pigeon cree in the country – built in the 1950s – is at Ryhope in Sunderland.

But be it leeks, dahlias or pigeons, what surrounds the pastimes is a sense of camaraderie and community which was the hallmark of mining settlements.

Tony Henderson, Environment Editor, The Journal, Newcastle

Tom Yellowley

Ned Taylor, head horse-keeper at Addison Colliery, near Ryton, in his greenhouse on Crookhill allotments c1970s.

The Big Meeting

'Lads unite and better your condition.'
Tommy Ramsey

George Robson, retired financial secretary of the Durham Area NUM, has been organiser of the annual Durham Miners' Gala for many years. The son of a Boldon Colliery pitman, George knows the history and details of the Gala inside out and his undimmed enthusiasm for the event is evident. He is an accomplished artist and a significant amount of his work is on the Gala theme.

This great event is an outpouring of the miners' spirit. It is famed throughout Britain and now almost legendary. The spirit of the pitmen and their communities has survived the decimation of the industry during the 1980s and 90s and the Gala goes from strength to strength despite the closure of the mines.

The Gala is the largest and most colourful miners' event in the world. It attracts visitors from many parts of the globe despite similar events elsewhere fading away after the pits closed. George Robson explains why former mining villages and towns in County Durham have rediscovered their heritage. 'With the closures, people in the villages began looking inward and asked themselves the question: "Why are we here?". The answer was: "Because of the pit." They decided to celebrate this fact.'

One of the most impressive developments has been the formation of groups to replicate or restore old lodge banners and parade them at the Gala and other events as symbols of pride in what the miners did for Britain and the world while

Durham Miners' Gala organiser and artist George Robson in his studio at Red Hills. He is the son of a Boldon Colliery miner.

Tom Yellowley

carrying out one of the most dangerous jobs imaginable. They are also symbols of the strong community spirit in villages and towns throughout the coalfield.

A considerable number of old banners are stored at Red Hills, the Durham union headquarters, and others are kept by the union lodges. The lodges help to continue the work of winning compensation for ex-miners affected by industrial diseases and injury.

George stresses the miners' record of concern for others. Contributions paid from their wages went into union welfare funds, both local and area-wide, for the benefit of many deserving causes, including hospitals and the Aged Miners' Homes. The good causes chosen to receive local funds were selected by the lodges and voted on by the membership.

The banner groups, supported by former pitmen, their families and others, show that the ethos of altruism and solidarity in the Durham coalfield is not dead. Every year, George is asked to arrange for new banners to be dedicated during the Miners' Festival Service at Durham Cathedral. This service is an important part of the cathedral's calendar and George liaises closely with the Dean and Chapter to make sure things run smoothly. The Bishop of Durham carries out the banner-blessing ceremony.

The cathedral contains a chapel dedicated to the Durham Light Infantry, complete with colours from the regiment's campaigns. Also in the cathedral is the Miners' Memorial, dedicated in 1947, which takes the form of an elaborate 17th century fireplace and includes the inscription: 'Remember before God the Durham Miners who have given their lives in the pits of this county and those who work in darkness and danger in those pits today.'

George felt that the fireplace was not perhaps the most beautiful tribute to those who campaigned in the coal mines of the county to win a war against underground dangers. He believed that a miners' banner would be a fitting, and more colourful, additional tribute. The Dean and Chapter agreed

George Robson

George Robson's painting of the NUM Durham Area banner at the Durham Gala.

to his request and today the Haswell Colliery banner is displayed opposite the DLI Chapel. Next to the fireplace, below a pit lamp, is the Miners' Book of Remembrance.

The Gala begins with miners, their families and friends assembling at Red Hills and at various other points on the periphery of central Durham. The bands, some of which come from beyond the Durham coalfield, including Yorkshire, march with the lodge banners, held proudly aloft by ex-miners and their families, into the city centre, reaching the County Hotel where the guest speakers and other leading figures stand on the balcony. Each band pauses to play for the speakers, before moving off along Old Elvet towards the former racecourse, where a funfair, the speeches and other events take place.

Before the speeches, the Mayor of Durham, accompanied by a ceremonial bodyguard, welcomes the men, women and children to the city. Robert Saint's famed miners' anthem, *Gresford*, is played in front of the platform by a chosen band.

The speeches on the racecourse have always been a central feature of the day. Many renowned Labour politicians and union leaders have addressed the Gala crowds.

The first Gala was held at Wharton Park, Durham, on August 12, 1871. It was essentially a mass demonstration of the miners' solidarity, intended to send a message to the employers that the men were united. About 4,000 to 5,000 pitmen and their families attended. Every Gala since then has been held at Durham's old racecourse.

The event has taken place each year since 1871, except during the two world wars, the lockout of 1921, in 1922, the Great Lockout of 1926 and the Great Strike of 1984-85. Attendances have varied, but the Gala always attracts many thousands. A record attendance of over 300,000 was reported in 1951. In some other years during the 1950s estimated attendances were around 200,000.

At the first 'Big Meeting', as the event came to be called, the platform was decorated with the banner of the Thornley Lodge of the Durham Miners' Association. Thornley was early a stronghold of mining trade unionism. In late 1843 men at this colliery went on strike against

excessive laying-out and fines, and were accused of breaking their Bond. They were cleared after a brilliant defence by W.P. Roberts. Another banner, in the arena, bore the message: 'A fair day's wage for a fair day's work.' A contest was held for the bands and various athletic sports took place.

Miners from 180 collieries attended the second Gala, in 1872. At this date the membership of the Durham union was around 35,000. The Big Meeting was addressed by Alexander McDonald, then president of the National Association of Miners, and by the Durham miners' pioneering leader William Crawford, who is credited with conceiving the idea of the Gala. He is likely to have looked back to the strikes of

Beamish Photographic Archive

Deaf Hill Temperance Band of miners with their lodge banner pose for a photograph at the Gala c1924.

1831, 1832 and 1844 when mass meetings with banners demonstrated the men's solidarity.

One of the resolutions passed by those present at the 1872 Gala stressed the importance of arbitration – a clear reference to the success of the union's talks with the employers earlier that year when the yearly Bond had been abolished and a 20% wage rise achieved.

The men have always remembered their fallen brothers. A tradition arose at the Gala of draping black crepe on a banner if one or more miners from that lodge had been killed in an accident during the year. That solemn rite of black crepe is still continued today if officials or other stalwarts of the lodge have passed away. The material was also draped on banners during funerals.

Red Hills, the Durham miners' union headquarters, which was opened in 1915.

George stresses that in the fight against large-scale pit closures, NUM president Arthur Scargill stated that it was not only jobs that were at stake, but also whole communities. Those communities suffered enormous hardship during the Great Strike in which the pitmen faced an intransigent and determined government led by Margaret Thatcher. They continue to suffer in various ways. The Gala has survived that unprecedented crisis against all the odds. So too has Red Hills, the Durham miners' fine headquarters, where the NUM continues the work of winning compensation for men suffering from conditions such as chronic bronchitis and emphysema and vibration white finger.

Early meetings of the Durham Miners' Association were held at the Market Tavern, Durham, and its first purpose-

149

built headquarters was opened in the city's North Road in 1875. The building was known as the Miners' Hall, and still stands, though it has been put to other uses. Its facade displayed statues of union pioneers, including William Crawford, the DMA's first leader, who became its president and general secretary. Also depicted in stone were Alexander Macdonald, the Scottish and national miners' leader and MP for Stafford, W.H. Patterson, who succeeded Crawford as DMA leader, and John Forman, who was an agent of the union, the name given to its most senior full-time officials, and served as president. Forman earned great respect by taking part in mine rescue work following disasters, including Seaham in 1880.

The Council Chamber at Red Hills, where delegates from the many lodges of the Durham Miners' Association met. Its curved, pew-like seating and windows are similar to those of a Methodist chapel. On this occasion a celebration has recently taken place, hence the balloons in the photograph.

The North Road building soon proved too small for large meetings of delegates from the lodges throughout County Durham and in the early 1900s it was decided that a new headquarters was needed. A site at Red Hills in Durham City was chosen and the DMA commissioned North East architect Henry Thomas Gradon to design a new miners' hall in which the union delegates could assemble together and which would contain committee rooms and offices for staff. Few could have been disappointed with the result.

Gradon created a magnificent building with a red and buff stone facade, arched lower windows and a green dome surmounting the building's profile. Constructed from the contributions of the pitmen, it was completed in 1915. The county's mines employed around 165,000 in 1913. Today, County Durham markets itself to tourists as 'Land of the Prince Bishops', yet it might just as appropriately be called 'Land of the Pitmen'.

Red Hills (officially known as Red Hill without the 's'), or the Miners' Hall as it is sometimes called, features a large, chapel-like Council Chamber for delegate meetings and conferences. George Robson describes this hall, where the miners' parliament met as the jewel in the crown of the headquarters.

The chamber is lined with oak panelling and can accommodate 300 delegates in curved rows of oak, pew-like seats. The overall effect is similar to that of a large Methodist chapel and this is hardly surprising considering the influence of Methodism among the early leaders. In this great room the council of the DMA met, which was formed from representatives of all the lodges. By the early 1900s there were almost 200 collieries in the county, but even this was not enough to produce sufficient delegates to fill the chamber to capacity.

Fittingly, a number of lodge banners hang in the corridors of Red Hills. One of these carries the words 'Compensation Day'. It is from Houghton lodge and depicts an injured miner and doctor and also two injured miners in a waiting room.

The atmosphere of the Muniment or Records Room on the upper floor of the building is charged with the spirit of past achievements and struggles. The room contains leather-bound volumes of the executive committee and council minutes. Its walls are adorned with numerous photographs of union leaders and other mementos.

On one of the walls is a sign of the union's contribution to victory in the Second World War – a plaque commemorating the pitmen's funding of two Spitfire aircraft. The union also paid for the provision of ambulances during the First World War.

On another wall is a large, full-length painting of Tommy Ramsey, a veteran of the 1844 strike who was a great recruiter for the union in the early days of the Durham

Tommy Ramsey with his crake (rattle). This fervent trade unionist helped to build up the Durham miners' union during its formative years. He visited the pit villages and towns, encouraging men to join the union and to attend meetings.

Miners' Association. In the face of opposition, he toured the mining villages with his crake (rattle), encouraging the men to attend meetings and join the union. Uttering slogans like 'Lads, unite and better your condition', he is remembered as a courageous man. According to John Wilson, on one occasion he was attacked by a 'bully' trying to curry favour with a manager. This man burnt his crake. However, Tommy acquired a new crake and 'turned it with more emphasis'.

The painting of Tommy shows him in top hat and holding his crake. The actual crake is displayed in a glass case close to the picture. Tommy died in 1873 and was buried at Blaydon Cemetery where his fine memorial takes the form of a statue with a canopy supported by pillars. He was undoubtedly one of the key men in building up the Durham union in its formative years.

Also on display in the Muniment Room are busts of Tommy Hepburn and Martin Jude. Hepburn, as we have seen, is recognised as the leading pioneer of mining trade unionism in the North East and Jude was another important leader in the early days of the movement, particularly during the strike of 1844.

Photographs on the walls include the First Labour Cabinet (1924) and a portrait of Bishop of Durham Brooke Foss Westcott, the 'Miners' Bishop'. The Muniment Room mirrors perfectly the proud history of the Durham miners' union.

Today, the NUM occupies only part of the main Red Hills building. The rest is now let out to charities and other organisations connected in some way to the aims and

The statue of William Crawford, first leader of the Durham Miners' Association, in the grounds of Red Hills.

aspirations of the union. Thompsons, the solicitors' firm specialising in employment law and industrial injuries and diseases, occupies offices in the building and works on behalf of the union to win compensation for ex-miners.

In the grounds, among the trees, there is a memorial garden to the men who died in the Easington and Eppleton disasters of 1951. There is also a plaque commemorating two of the last miners to be killed in the Durham coalfield – at Wearmouth Colliery in February 1992. These men, Gerard Sumby and Eric Evans, were involved in a transport accident. The inscription on the plaque makes clear that this is also a memorial to all workers killed each year in the UK in the course of their employment.

The garden features art works with a mining theme, including a sculpture of a miner lifting a derailed tub. It is entitled *The Putter*. The sculptor was former miner Brian Brown. Another work depicts a pony and tub.

The gates of Red Hills are flanked by pillars topped by stone figures of miners with picks. The tall, imposing statues from the old North Road building line one side of the driveway. The impressive figures of Crawford, Patterson, Macdonald and Forman look across the central area of the garden, keeping watch over the movement they helped to shape.

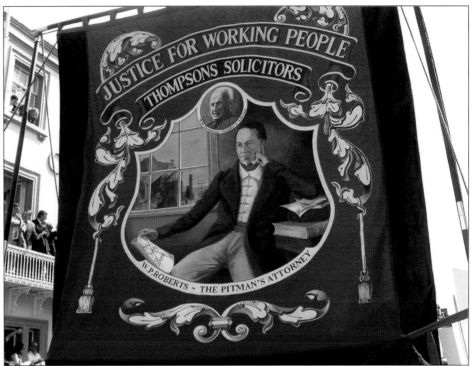

Thompsons Solicitors

The banner of Thompsons Solicitors, who specialise in industrial injuries, diseases and employment law, at the Durham Miners' Gala. The banner carries a portrait of W.P. Roberts, the 'Pitman's Attorney'. He successfully defended miners in the Monkwearmouth Bond case of 1869, a catalyst which led to the foundation of the Durham Miners' Association.

Banners to the Racecourse

The Big Meeting, July 2007

We drive to Durham early on a cloudy morning in July 2007 for the 123rd Miners' Gala. George Robson greets us at Red Hills where already – at just after 8am – former miners and other trade unionists are assembling their banners in the grounds and various bands are gathering.

The gatehouse at Red Hills is a hive of activity – it is the office of Durham Colliery Mechanics. Jim Perry, administrator of the Mechanics, is helping to assemble its banner which has just been attached to the poles. It bears the motto: 'The past we inherit, the future we build.'

In the lane outside the gates – Flass Street – the NUM North East Area Band is already lining up in front of the Area banner which is held high. They are to lead the march to the old racecourse, the first of an 'army' of colourful bands and banners which for the next four or more hours will parade through streets of the venerable old city.

Behind the band, a group of men from the Bevin Boys Association gather to take their place as second in the parade. They hold a green banner. Some of these wartime miners have journeyed from as far as the South Coast to be here. They make the pilgrimage to Durham each year.

Suddenly the bass drum of the Area Band sounds out with a loud pounding and then the other musicians raise their brass instruments to their lips. The sounds of cornets, baritones, euphoniums, trombones and tubas carry down towards the city centre. The march has started.

Richard Smith

The NUM North East Area Band march through Durham City at the 2007 Gala.

It is an extraordinary moment. As we march with the Area banner fluttering in the wind our feelings are almost impossible to describe. We are taking part in an event which captures, like no other, the spirit of the miners and their communities. It is an uplifting experience to step out along the streets where so many pitmen have marched in the past, shoulder to shoulder, to show their solidarity. We are deeply moved to be a part of this lasting tradition.

One side of the banner depicts Red Hills, Durham Cathedral, the Tyne Bridge and St Nicholas Cathedral in Newcastle – County Durham and Northumberland united – together with roundel portraits of Tommy Hepburn and Martin Jude and images of miners' lamps. The motto reads: 'United we stand – divided we fall'.

Crowds are already forming to watch the parade as we cross Framwellgate Bridge with the sun breaking through. The band crosses the Market Square in the city centre. Ironically, the marchers pass the equestrian statue of the 3rd Marquess of Londonderry in military uniform. But it is the miners and their Gala which hold the attention of the thickening crowds, not the marquess. Soon we are crossing Elvet Bridge. A glance behind shows that we have been joined by other bands and banners. Standing out, behind the Bevin Boys, is the Craghead Lodge banner with its colourful yellow background. It bears portraits of 'Three Men of Merit' – Clement Attlee, Aneurin Bevan and Arthur Horner (a former president of the NUM).

Beyond the bridge lies the historic thoroughfare of Old Elvet. The Area Band halts to play in front of the County Hotel where the speakers and union leaders stand on the balcony, enjoying the music and smiling.

Up Old Elvet we march, the band playing tirelessly, and then we turn down towards the old racecourse. Dotting the

The Craghead Lodge banner rests on the Gala field with band instruments in the foreground in July 2007. It bears the portraits of Clement Attlee, Aneurin Bevan and Arthur Horner – 'Three Men of Merit'.

edges of the field are numerous tents, stalls and fairground rides.

It is not long before other bands and banners appear at the top of the slope. The succession of lodges takes several hours to pass down on to the racecourse. Among the first are Craghead and Springwell. The Springwell banner carries the message 'Unity is Strength.' Also early on the field is the handsome scarlet banner of Wheatley Hill Lodge bearing the unmistakable portrait of miners' leader Peter Lee. The other side features a Biblical scene with the quotation: 'Suffer the little children to come unto me'.

Silksworth's banner carries a pithead scene, complete with winding wheels, Esh Winning's features the message: 'All men are brethren', East Hetton's, generally known as Kelloe, depicts the Good Samaritan with the parable's message: 'Go thou and do likewise.' The Murton Lodge banner bears a socialist motto: 'Production for use, not for profit.' The other side carries a large portrait of Tommy Hepburn. Several banners show Durham Cathedral and Conishead Priory as well as various groups of Aged Miners' Homes.

Also on the field are the standards of the Durham Aged Mineworkers' Homes Association, bearing the portraits of John Wilson and Joseph Hopper, and Thompsons Solicitors, which carries a painting of 'Pitman's Attorney' W.P. Roberts.

Meanwhile, the racecourse has been filling up with happy people of all ages. A considerable number of musicians in the bands are under the age of 20. Eventually, the sound of a band playing *Gresford* is heard and the speakers and other guests appear on the platform near the centre of the field.

At 3pm, the Miners' Festival Service is held in Durham Cathedral. The link between the pitmen and the cathedral is a strong one. A senior cleric is on Palace Green to welcome

Richard Smith

The Springwell Lodge DMA banner is carried on to the old racecourse, displaying the portraits of past leaders.

the three bands and four banners. Two of the banners, those of Greenside and Deaf Hill, are new and are to be dedicated by the Bishop.

The service is packed with people – it is difficult to find a seat. The Bishop of Durham, Tom Wright, the Dean, Michael Sadgrove, and other clerics stand at the head of the nave, awaiting the banners. Then, muffled notes are heard which grow louder. The NUM North East Area Band enters

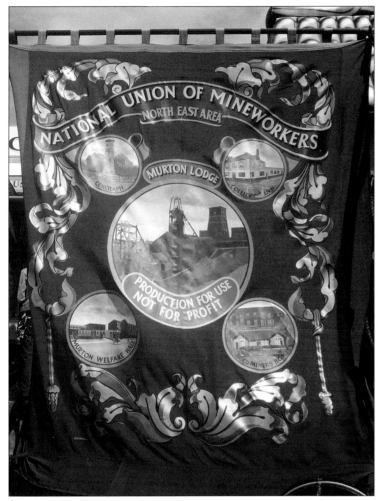

Richard Smith

Richard Smith

The Silksworth Lodge NUM banner reaches the Gala field.

The Murton Lodge NUM banner bears the motto 'Production for Use Not for Profit' and a central picture of the colliery.

through the main door of the cathedral and proceeds slowly up the aisle, playing softly, followed closely by their banner and the Deaf Hill banner. Afterwards, the two other bands and banners enter. Bishop Tom dedicates and blesses the new banners and after the blessing, the Area Band plays *Gresford*.

The sermon is delivered by Canon David Kennedy, who was brought up in South Shields and recalls the pits of his home town – Harton and Westoe. Canon Kennedy describes Durham Cathedral as 'The Miners' Cathedral'. At the end, the bands march out to lively tunes with the congregation clapping in time, giving them a rousing send off. The great cathedral is filled with the spirit of the pitmen.

The 69th Bishop of Durham, David Jenkins, was enthroned during the Great Strike of 1984-85. Britain's

Richard Smith

The Durham Colliery Mechanics' standard, with its picture of Durham Cathedral.

Richard Smith

The NUM North East Area Band march to Durham Cathedral for the annual Miners' Festival Service in 2007.

miners were fighting mass pit closures. In his enthronement sermon, before a congregation of over 2,000 people, Dr Jenkins urged compromise by both sides in the dispute and declared that the 'miners must not be defeated' – yet, he pointed out, the government seemed determined to achieve their defeat. 'The cost of hope in our society and in our politics is a responsible readiness for compromise,' he said.

He spoke of the desperation of the miners for the welfare and future of their communities. This had driven them to the action they were now taking. No one should forget what it meant to be a part of a community centred on a mine or works when that mine or works closed. 'It is death, depression and desolation,' he declared. 'A society which seeks economic progress for material ends must not indifferently exact such human suffering from some for the sake of the affluence of others.'

Turning to the Conservative government under Prime Minister Margaret Thatcher, Bishop Jenkins said they seemed to be indifferent to 'poverty and powerlessness'. Their financial policies had consistently improved the lot of the already better off. He added that the government's answer to civil unrest seemed to be to make the means of suppression more efficient, while ignoring or playing down the causes.

The friendly relationship between the Durham miners and clerics of Durham Cathedral had its beginnings in 1892 when Bishop Brooke Foss Westcott interceded between the pitmen and employers during a major strike against a wage reduction. He asked both sides to the Bishop's residence, Auckland Palace, where he urged a settlement of their differences.

The two parties first held a joint meeting and then split up to meet in separate rooms. According to John Wilson (*A History of the Durham Miners' Association 1870-1904*) 'the bishop passed from room to room full of solicitude for a settlement'. Although the strike failed to achieve its original objective, the amiable cleric was dubbed 'The Miners' Bishop' for his efforts. He had succeeded in persuading the owners to drop their demand for a 13.5% reduction in wages. Instead, the cut was lowered to 10%. This was the percentage which the owners had originally demanded. While the strike was in progress they had raised their demand to 13.5%.

In 1896, Bishop Westcott invited the pitmen and their families to take part in a Gala Day service at the cathedral, so beginning this well-loved and well-attended annual event.

A veteran Greenside miner, enjoying the occasion, stands in front of his colliery's banner outside Durham Cathedral, 2007.
The banner was among two dedicated that year at the Miners' Festival Service.

A Special Picnic

'One miner helped the other.'
George Brown

The men north of the Tyne had their own special gathering, the Northumberland Miners' Picnic. It was first held on June 11, 1866, on land between Bog Houses and Shankhouse, now part of the north-eastern edge of Cramlington. However, Carlisle Park in Morpeth and, later, Ashington and Bedlington, were among the venues for the event over the many years which followed, with Bedlington eventually becoming the favourite. Many of the early Picnics took place on the Northumberland coast at Blyth Links, and inland at Morpeth, with several others being held in Newcastle and at Tynemouth.

The Picnic became an annual fixture like the Durham Gala and it too was an occasion for demonstrating the comradeship and brotherly feeling of the miners as well as the friendly spirit and closeness of their communities. Also like the Gala, it was a day out for the pitmen, their wives and families, a welcome break from their hard working lives.

Accompanied by branch banners, the colliery bands would march to the picnic field. Before the march the bands competed for honours in an annual contest. A picnic beauty queen was chosen to grace the proceedings and families sat down to an open-air meal on the grass. The miners often enjoyed beers with their marras.

As in Durham, it was an occasion for the people from the many pit villages of Northumberland to meet, mingle, exchange stories and experiences and renew friendships or make new ones.

William Ward

Miners and their families with the West Sleekburn NUM branch banner march through Bedlington at the Northumberland Miners' Picnic in 1954.

Political speeches, with union leaders and politicians addressing the crowd from the platform, were as much a part of the Picnic as they were of the Gala. The banners, held aloft with pride, reflected in their motifs and slogans heartfelt hopes of a better future for the miner and his family

– a future of fair wages, adequate compensation and a decent home in old age. Some also carried a message of solidarity, of the need for unity.

George Brown, of Bedlington Station, worked as a miner at Ellington Colliery from 1938 to 1966 and played euphonium in the colliery band. He started off as a cornet player at the age of 12 in 1936. The band was known as the Lynemouth Silver Band in those days, but changed its name to the Ellington Colliery Band after nationalisation in 1947. From 1937, George played at the Northumberland Miners' Picnic many times. He also played with the Newbiggin band.

Winning the championship at the Picnic was a prestigious achievement. Before the Second World War each member of the winning band received a medal. Ellington and North Seaton are two of the bands that George remembers enjoying the most success in the contest. Other bands enjoying considerable success included Cowpen and Crofton, and Backworth.

As well as a cash prize for the overall winner, awards were made to individual players. In 1955, George became the first musician to receive the Rose Bowl, the Dunsmoor Trophy, for best euphonium. He put in much hard work to achieve this honour, practising for hours after coming home from his shift at the mine. His father was also a pitman at Ellington and died from pneumoconiosis. He played cornet in the Barrington Colliery band.

Despite a considerable amount of drinking most of the Picnics George attended were very peaceful affairs. The Picnic was a much smaller event than the Gala, but of great social importance to the Northumberland miners. George

Ellington Colliery bandsman George Brown with his wife Jean and son Colin at the Northumberland Miners' Picnic at Bedlington in 1955. In front is the trophy George won for euphonium playing.

remembers that the march to and from the field would feature about 15 colliery banners, far less than in Durham which had many more pits.

George recalls a shift in the 1950s when one of his marras nearly lost his life. A large section of stone collapsed on top of him. 'It was over most of his body. You could only see his head.' George and other men had to use equipment to lift the massive stone before pulling his friend out. He had suffered serious injuries to both legs.

George himself received a bad ankle injury during his mining days and this still gives him problems. He also suffered injuries to both knees.

Former miner John Douds, of Seaton Sluice, carried the

Bedlington A Pit banner at the Picnic of 1970, the year before this colliery closed. He found it exhilarating as the crowds cheered and people danced in front of the banner. His group set off from outside the Bedlington A pithead baths at Bedlington Station and marched over a mile to the centre of Bedlington. Afterwards they paraded down to the Picnic area in the town's Attlee Park. John describes the Picnic as the highlight of the year. In Bedlington the town centre forms a natural amphitheatre, so people were able to get a great view of the banners and bands.

But things have changed. Today, with no deep mines left, the Picnic takes the form of a miners' memorial service and a lecture meeting with various speakers. Deborah Welch, of Northumberland Area NUM, organises this event. 'There is no Picnic as such but people still call it that,' she says.

A newly-made Northumberland Area NUM banner, a 'first' for the whole Area, was dedicated at the Woodhorn museum in March 2007. It was the result of a joint project between the NUM, the Northumberland Aged Mineworkers' Homes Association and Northumberland County Council with the help of the Heritage Lottery Fund.

The new banner was inspired by one dating from the early 1920s carried by miners of the Ashington Group of Collieries. On one side it features what is perhaps the strongest imagery of any throughout the Great Northern Coalfield. A group of miners carry a coffin in a funeral

Ellington Colliery Band members pose for a picture with the championship trophy, which they have won, the Burt Challenge Cup, at the Northumberland Miners' Picnic at Bedlington in 1954. The Ellington branch banner is behind.

procession from a colliery. Some of the men are injured. The pit is on fire. However, emerging from the blazing pit shaft is the giant figure of a man who is pointing a spear labelled 'State Control' towards a fire-breathing dragon symbolising profit and private ownership. The man is clearly about to slay the dragon of capitalism.

The message on the banner reads: 'The workers' industrial union and his own political Labour Party will destroy this monster.' It is a call for common ownership of the mines, indicating that health and safety should be put before profit.

The other side features the words 'The New Vision' with a female figure carrying a torch as she leads workmen, including a miner in shorts, towards a group of children dancing around a maypole with the words 'Gain the Co-operative Commonwealth' above them. The maypole ribbons bear the words 'Beauty, Fellowship, Health, Art and Science'. This extraordinary icon of mining trade unionism is now kept at the headquarters of Northumberland Area NUM.

Young people were involved in the project which led to the creation of the new banner. As a means of encouraging them to appreciate their unique cultural heritage and embrace the old 'coalfield community spirit' the Northumberland Area of the NUM, the Aged Mineworkers' Homes Association and Northumberland County Council formed a partnership to deliver the 'Northumberland Miners' Banner Project' financed by

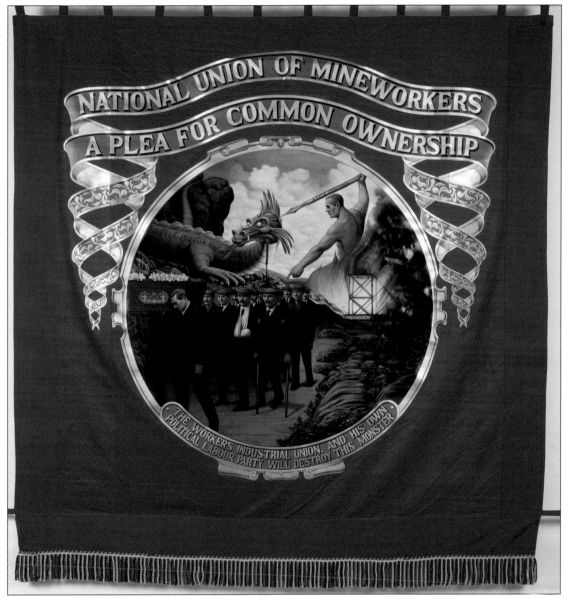

The new Northumberland Area NUM banner, a replication of a 1920s banner of the Ashington Group of collieries' miners. The dragon represents private ownership and the giant man emerging from the blazing pit symbolises common ownership.

Heritage Lottery Fund. The project meant that ex-miners met and talked to the youngsters about what life was like in the old pit communities and working down the mines. They visited Beamish Museum where they were able to see some of the old banners. This inspired the design of the new banner which uses the same stunning imagery and delivers the same strong messages in support of the working man and his family.

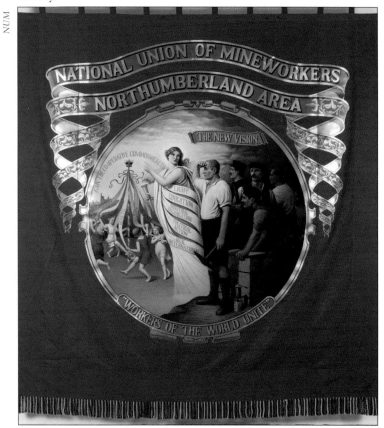

The other side of the Northumberland Area NUM banner. A pitman in hoggers, shorts and carrying a pick, together with other workers, is being led by a female figure towards the 'New Vision' of the 'Co-operative Commonwealth.'

The colourful banners carried at the Durham Gala, the Northumberland Picnic, at funerals, during strikes, demonstrations and other events illustrate the spirit and values of the miners. They are painted on both sides with themes and mottoes or quotations, all reflecting the essentially humanitarian values of the miner and his community. They are both moving and inspiring, displaying the strong influences of Christianity, socialist ideals and trade unionism. Here is a vision which transcends narrow materialism.

The banners, representing the different union lodges or branches, were in earlier years made from silk. When a banner became worn, it was replaced by another and so during the history of a lodge several were produced.

A Yugoslavian diplomat who attended the memorial service for the Easington Colliery disaster victims in 1951 attached a pennant version of his country's flag to a wreath on one of the coffins. It was a mark of respect which did not go unnoticed. From then onwards, the pitmen of Easington draped the Yugoslav pennant over their own lodge banner at the Big Meeting in acknowledgement of that moving tribute.

Among the surviving Northumberland NUM banners is one from Bedlington Doctor Pit which carries on one side the figure of a miner looking towards the sky which features the word 'Socialism'. Below him are the words: 'Prosperity and happiness – Health and peace – Five day week – Nationalisation – Family Allowances – Social Security.' The other side shows a miner and his family looking up at an angel in the sky representing the Labour Party.

The theme of public ownership is also taken up by an Ashington NUM banner of 1949. A miner and his family, his wife in stiletto heels, are seen looking towards a pithead with the word 'Nationalisation' above it. The other side features

William Ward

Marching with the Cambois banner at the 1955 Picnic.

views of the five collieries in the Ashington Group. Ashington is in the middle, the others being Ellington, Woodhorn, Linton and Lynemouth.

An Ellington NUM branch banner of 1950 carries scenes by Oliver Kilbourn, a member of the Ashington Group of painters. One side shows a sombre view of colliery housing seen through the frame of a pit ventilation door, which is about to close. The motto reads: 'Close the door on past dreariness.' The other side depicts new homes in a bright tree-lined street, seen through the open door, with the words: 'Open it to future brightness.'

A Pegswood branch banner depicts a crowd of people around a pithead on the day Britain's mines were nationalised. It carries the words 'Vesting Day, Jan 1st 1947.' One of the buildings shown has a notice which reads: 'This colliery is managed by the NCB on behalf of the people.' The other side carries a central portrait of William Straker, a former general secretary of the Northumberland miners' union. He is surrounded by portraits of Keir Hardie, Robert Smillie, Emanuel Shinwell and A.J. Cook. The message reads: 'They blazed the trail.' Many of the Northumberland banners are now kept at the Woodhorn Museum and Archives Centre in Ashington.

Spirit of the miners in music

The music of colliery brass bands helped to strengthen the solidarity of the pitmen in times of dispute and acted as a solace in times of hardship and ordeal. Indeed, bands are still a central feature of the Durham Miners' Gala and were also a crucial part of the Northumberland Miners' Picnic.

Hebburn Colliery Band was one of many in the Great Northern Coalfield. It was also among the most exceptional. The Hebburn band hit the headlines in 1904 when it won the prestigious Crystal Palace 1,000 Guineas Trophy and the national championship. It was an award regarded as the FA Cup in the world of brass band contests.

The Chopwell Colliery Band at the Durham Miners' Gala in 1920. The famed Chopwell Lodge 'Red Banner' forms a backdrop.

Among the musicians from Hebburn was composer Robert Saint who was born in Hebburn to a mining family. In 1936 he wrote the miners' hymn, *Gresford*. This moving anthem of the pitmen is always played at the Durham Miners' Gala, and was first performed there in 1938. *Gresford* commemorates the 266 miners who died in the Gresford Colliery disaster, near Wrexham, North Wales, in 1934. Bob Saint, as he was known on Tyneside, was a miner at Hebburn Colliery until its closure in 1931.

Another group which achieved great success was the St Hilda Colliery Band, of South Shields. It won the Crystal Palace trophy three times – in 1912, 1920 and 1921. Also of renown was South Moor Colliery Silver Prize Band which captured the Grand Shield at the Crystal Palace contest in 1907. Harton Colliery Band added to the North East's honours by winning the British Open Musical Competition in 1919.

A considerable number of the North East bands which play today at the Gala and Picnic can trace their origins to the collieries. They include the award-winning Fishburn Band and the Backworth Colliery Band. The last group of musicians to be attached to a working deep mine in the region was the Ellington Colliery Band, Northumberland. Following closure of the pit, this group was sponsored by Northumbrian Water and continues as the Northumbrian Water Ellington Colliery Band.

The fight for compensation

In a message to those attending the 2007 Gala, Dave Guy, president of the NUM North East Area and the Durham Miners' Association, reported that since the previous Gala they had recovered £23.2m in compensation awards for men with Vibration White Finger (VWF) and Chronic Bronchitis and Emphysema (CBE). This made a total of £207m recovered since the Durham Miners first brought a test case for VWF in the early 1990s. He praised the work of the union's solicitors, Thompsons, in fighting for this compensation.

Mr Guy wrote: 'It is almost unbelievable that it was not until 1979 that the men suffering from miners' disease pneumoconiosis (black lung) received lump-sum compensation. This was to a large extent as a result of a case won by our solicitors Thompsons in 1956. This case established that if as a result of negligence by an employer a worker contracted a disease, then the employer was liable to pay compensation.'

He pointed out that in 1998 the Durham Miners and Mechanics won a number of test cases in the High Court which established that miners suffering from VWF were due compensation. Legislation establishing compensation for miners suffering from CBE caused by exposure to dust was established in 1993, but Mr Guy added that 'the union had to fight against all the obstacles and delays engineered by the Department of Trade and Industry'. Compensation has been won for thousands of miners and their dependants, but many more claims still have to be settled.

Tom Yellowley

A Houghton Lodge DMA banner depicts injured miners and a doctor on 'Compensation Day.' It was made by George Tutill of London, one of the best known banner manufacturers.

The Great Strike 1984-85

'The enemy within.'
Margaret Thatcher

The Great Strike of 1984-85 was an epic battle between the Conservative government, led by Margaret Thatcher, and Britain's miners, led by NUM president Arthur Scargill. It was a confrontation like no other. It seems the government believed that if it defeated the miners – the workers with the greatest solidarity – it would have defeated the entire British trade union movement.

By the early 1970s miners' pay had fallen behind the levels for workers in many other sectors of industry. Pay was now considered low and men felt it was time for action to close the gap. Following rejection of a 'meagre' pay offer from the NCB, a national miners' strike was staged in 1972 in an attempt to 'catch up' on the wages front. Coal stocks dwindled and power cuts resulted. The strike was successful in winning increases.

In 1973, a move by the pitmen to improve their pay still further led to an overtime ban and the government took the counter-measure of putting industry on a three-day week in a bid to avoid power cuts. The miners then voted to strike in early 1974 and this resulted in a general election at which Edward Heath's Conservative government was defeated and Labour elected. Mr Heath had fought the election on the question of 'Who governs the country?'

Following the 'Winter of Discontent' in 1978-79, when strikes took place across several sectors of employment, a Conservative government was returned to office under a new leader, Margaret Thatcher. She was no friend of the unions.

Numerous pit closures had occurred throughout the 1960s, including during Labour's term in government, and some in the early 1970s, but it was the Conservative government's accelerated closures programme of the 1980s which set alarm bells ringing in the mining communities. By this time, a situation had been reached where shutdowns on a large-scale would potentially threaten the life of those communities. Accelerated closures meant the accelerated decline of Britain's coal industry and of the pit villages and towns.

In 1982, Arthur Scargill revealed a leaked National Coal Board (NCB) document showing large-scale pit closures were planned over the next decade. The following year the NCB refused to agree to wage talks with the NUM unless the miners accepted closures and job cuts. The miners reacted with an overtime ban, starting in November 1983. The NCB revealed that it was planning to close 20 pits in the following year with the loss of around 20,000 jobs. It was reported that the plan would reduce production in Northumberland and Durham by over one million tonnes. Northumberland Area NUM president Denis Murphy said: 'One thing is clear and that is the North is expected to take the largest cut in production of anywhere in the country.'

Early in 1984, the NCB announced plans to shut three collieries within five weeks without going through the review procedure. This seemed to many people to be indecent haste. These were Cortonwood Colliery in South Yorkshire where

ncjMedia / The Journal

A confrontation between picketing miners and police officers at Ellington Colliery during the 1984-85 strike. The stoppage lasted a year.

balloting led to strike action, starting on March 5, one in Scotland and another in Kent. The NUM National Executive Committee then backed a national strike against the closures, and a delegate conference of the union called on all miners to join the stoppage. The strike quickly spread to all areas. Flying pickets from Yorkshire and Scotland visited the North East to encourage resistance to the closures.

Shortly before the strike began, an incident occurred at Ellington Colliery in Northumberland which made national headlines. NCB chairman Ian MacGregor fell to the ground when a crowd of protesting miners surged towards him. He was visiting the colliery to meet officials after announcing the planned closures and job losses.

Arthur Scargill emphasised that the shutdowns programme threatened both miners' jobs and their communities. The threat to the communities went hand in hand with the threat to jobs. The closure of a village or town's mine was a grievous blow to the life of that community. It meant not only economic depression and demoralisation, but also the potential collapse of a way of life. The sons of miners, unable to find work in the pit community or nearby, would move away.

The reaction of the government was to launch a huge police operation nationwide to render mass picketing ineffective. Such picketing was said by ministers to be a way of preventing men from exercising their right to work. Significantly, of course, effective picketing would mean the likely defeat of the NCB plan for large-scale closures.

The government pointed out that there had been no national secret ballot and contended that the stoppage was undemocratic. Ministers exploited this aspect of the dispute to full effect in the media. Yet many in the NUM believed it would be unfair for a miner at a pit not under threat to decide the fate of another man whose pit was facing closure. In the event, the majority of miners supported the strike in response to the call from their delegates nationwide. It is highly likely therefore that a national ballot would have confirmed this support.

Mrs Thatcher saw the miners and their leaders as 'the enemy within'. The miners perceived their strike as a fight for jobs, their way of life and their communities. It appeared that the prime minister was consigning men who had braved their lives in the pits to the status of outlaws.

The defeat of Edward Heath's government at the polls in 1974 must have strongly influenced the thinking of ministers. In addition, the view of Baldwin and Churchill during the General Strike, that the miners, and in particular their leaders, were in some way a threat to the State and constitution, still seemed to permeate Conservative attitudes in the 1980s. The 45 years during which pitmen had worked without a national strike, from 1926 to 1972, including the Second World War, were unrecognised or overlooked. In 1972-74 they acted to defend their living standards which they had perceived to be slipping. Now, in 1984 they were acting to preserve their jobs, communities and way of life.

Harrowing events were to take place which left a legacy of bitterness. Miners picketing collieries encountered large numbers of police officers wearing helmets, visors and carrying battons and riot shields. It seemed an extraordinary reaction to a strike. Thousands of miners were arrested. The most intense confrontation between police and strikers took place at Orgreave Colliery, South Yorkshire, in June 1984 where mounted police and dogs were deployed. Mr Scargill was among those arrested.

A proportion of miners were unhappy that no pithead ballots had been called, although under NUM rules this was

ncjMedia / The Journal

Members of the Blyth Miners' Wives Support Group on a sponsored march from Blyth to Bedlington to raise money for the striking pitmen's families in June 1984. Accompanying them on the walk were around 20 pitmen from Bates Colliery with their banner. On reaching Bedlington, the marchers joined a rally of Northumberland miners, which was held instead of the annual Picnic.

not necessarily required. In Durham, an executive committee meeting recommended strike action by a 5-3 vote. However, the Area Council was split 7-7 on the issue. Durham NUM president Harold Mitchell then used his casting vote in favour of strike action in support of the Yorkshire and Scottish miners without a ballot. The decision was reached following the refusal of NCB area director David Archibald to give an assurance there would be 'no more closures'.

At 12 of the North East's 20 collieries the miners were reported to be in favour of strike action. The remaining eight were against. Soon, however, the entire Great Northern Coalfield was halted, with flying pickets bringing Dawdon and Ashington to a standstill by mid-March.

Brenkley, in the Northumberland coalfield, was the only colliery left in operation at this time. It seems this drift mine escaped the attention of flying pickets from Durham simply because they could not find it, tucked away as it was across fields to the west of Seaton Burn. It was, however, eventually located.

In late March, miners virtually halted coal supplies to Blyth Power Station. There were 24 arrests. The workers at the plant agreed to strictly enforce their union rules and refuse entry to non-union lorry drivers.

In early April, the Durham coalfield's oldest surviving and smallest pit, Bearpark, closed after 110 years. Amidst all the angst of the dispute, the union held a closing down party in the village club with management invited along. The pit was exhausted and the men had accepted closure as inevitable. They nevertheless gave full support to their brother miners in opposing further shutdowns.

The battle to save the pits raged on. As in 1926, the pitmen and their families faced great hardship, but the women of the coalfields backed their men, forming support groups and taking an active part in the campaign to stop closures. Without this support, it is doubtful if the miners could have held out as long as they did.

Blow after blow fell upon the men and their families and upon the NUM. The miners were denied social security benefits for joining a strike which the government were determined to defeat. Supplementary benefit payments to their families were reduced. In September 1984, the High Court ordered the assets of the NUM to be sequestered. The union went into receivership.

The strikers were further weakened by the failure of the pit deputies' union, the National Association of Colliery Overmen, Deputies and Shotfirers (NACODS) to join the stoppage, although they had wavered on this issue and most deputies strongly sympathised with the men on strike. Indeed, at one point they had voted to join the strike. In addition, many – though not all – pitmen in Nottinghamshire opposed the stoppage, opening up a rift in the ranks. This engendered bitterness. As in the past, to be a blackleg was anathema.

Lack of a national ballot, the deployment of unprecedented numbers of police, the existence of large stockpiles of coal and the stance taken by NACODS were important factors in eroding the miners' position. There seems little doubt the government had prepared carefully for this battle.

The dispute dragged on through the winter of 1984-85, the miners having adopted the slogan 'Coal Not Dole'. The Great Strike was to last almost exactly a year, five months longer than the 1926 lockout. Indeed, industrial action, from the overtime ban starting in November 1983, lasted 16 months.

Christopher Wood, of South Shields, was aged 14 when

ncjMedia / The Journal

the miners' strike began. He remembers: 'I was attending Westoe Comprehensive School. The strike holds particularly strong memories for me due to the location of the school, which faced directly on to the main gates of Westoe Colliery. Two members of my family, my brother and uncle, who lived with us, worked at the pit and came out when the strike was called.

'Right from the start there was trouble on the picket lines. Many a time our lessons were disrupted as miners and police clashed at the gates when the 'scab buses' with grille windows entered the colliery.

Happier days. Pitmen sit in electric cars to ride down the Havannah Drift mine in February 1975. The 570 men employed at this colliery had recently broken a production record. The mine was situated near the western end of Coach Lane, Dinnington, not far from Newcastle Airport's runways and to the south-east of Dinnington Village. The site is now occupied by a few industrial buildings and the Havannah Nature Reserve.

One of the school's buildings overlooked the entrance to the pit and on each occasion these confrontations occurred most of the class would rush to the windows to see what was going on.' Chris noticed that with the 'so-called drift back to work' during the winter months the confrontations became more frequent and more intense.

'Initially we managed okay, but as the strike dragged on my family (as many others did) started to encounter problems. As money became tighter, we began to rely more and more on food parcels donated to the miners. Ex-miners gave these to us and they consisted of basic items such as tea, sugar, bread etc. We also received food parcels from the then communist states, such as Bulgarian jam, Polish sugar and other tinned and jarred foodstuffs from the Eastern bloc countries.

'As the strike continued my family's financial position became more strained and as a result of not being able to pay our telephone bill our phone was cut off immediately.'

Chris added: 'Whilst the strike ended in 1985 much of the ill feeling still continues today towards those who went back during the dispute. Indeed, I have heard of numerous incidents from family and friends of strike breakers still encountering trouble from a dispute which ended over 20 years ago.'

A former miner at Bates Colliery, Blyth, recalls the strike vividly. 'I picketed at Bates, Ellington, Whittle and Wearmouth and also at Lancaster Docks. Blacklegs were brought in by bus and there was a lot of pushing and shoving in an attempt to stop them. The windows of the buses were covered with wire mesh. You couldn't see who was inside. The drivers wore balaclavas.' At Wearmouth, mounted police officers were on duty.

He said that as the stoppage entered its last few months men began drifting back to work, the largest number returning after the failure of NACODS to support the strike. 'If NACODS had joined us every pit in the country would have been stopped.'

He remembers the miners' wives and the NUM organising a soup kitchen at Cowpen & Crofton Welfare, where meals were served. A van would call at the Welfare on a Friday to sell eggs and potatoes at cut prices.

Times were desperate. His main concern was to feed and clothe his wife and children. He and many other pitmen would search for old metal such as aluminium, brass or copper and sell it to scrap yards. Beaches were combed for coal. Occasionally they might be given vouchers for food, clothing and shoes for their children by county council social services. The money, he says, was claimed back by the council after the end of the dispute.

On March 3, 1985, one of the longest stoppages in British trade union history ended when NUM delegates at a national conference voted by a small majority for a return to work without reaching an agreement with the NCB. The wonder was that the miners had held out so long against the overwhelming forces drawn up against them. Even so, displaying a resilient spirit, North East pitmen marched proudly back to work with their banners to the fore.

Within a decade most of the country's deep mines would be shut down, the industry contracting to just a few pits. Black diamonds were increasingly imported from abroad. The British coal industry had been reduced to near extinction by government policy.

We Were Eating Dust

'There were no other people like pitmen.'
Jim Wilson

Wearmouth Colliery, also known as Monkwearmouth, on the northern bank of the River Wear in Sunderland, closed in December 1993. It was a modern, undersea mine. Sunderland AFC's Stadium of Light opened on the site of the former pit in 1997. Crowds of football supporters cheer on their team where once miners emerged 'into the light' from beneath the ground, blackened and exhausted from their shift. Many of those cheering supporters worked in the mines of the area. Indeed, the reference to light recalls the colliery – a giant Davy lamp stands close to the ticket office.

Retired miner Jim Wilson, of Usworth, Washington, worked in the pits of the area for 30 years, including Wearmouth. At his home, a deputy's safety lamp adorns the hearth. His mantlepiece features the coaly figurine of a miner. On the walls are pictures of NUM lodge banners – Monkwearmouth, Glebe, Washington F and Usworth. One side of the Monkwearmouth banner carries a painting of the court scene which led to the cancellation of the Bond at the colliery in 1869. The motto reads: 'Come, let us reason together.' The other side declares: 'In God is all our trust.'

A slogan on the Usworth banner strikes a more militant tone, quoting Karl Marx and Frederich Engels: 'Workers of the world unite, you have nothing to lose but your chains.

Jimmy Wilson

Wearmouth Colliery, pictured shortly before final demolition. The pit closed in late 1993. It was the last deep mine in the Durham coalfield.

You have a world to win.' It also displays the words: 'Emancipation of Labour.' Glebe's message reads: 'Unity is Strength.'

On the landing at the top of Jim's stairs a painting depicts England's last pit pony, Flax of Ellington, accompanied by a miner. 'I can tell you the names of every face I worked on,' says Jim, who served at Glebe, Usworth, Boldon and Wearmouth. He did his face training at Westoe. Jim retired from mining after Wearmouth closed. He says: 'The only thing I miss is the people and I haven't heard a good joke for years. There were no other people like pitmen.'

Jim continues: 'I started work at the Glebe Colliery in 1967 when I was 15. My token number at the Glebe was 245. When I first started my pay was £6.9s.6d and I had £5.10s to draw. I used to answer to three names: the ones who knew my grandad would call me Dick, the ones who knew my dad would call me Alec, and my own age would obviously call me Jim.

'I first worked on the screens at bank and when I was 16 I was at the shaft bottom. I was 18 when I went on the faces, in the 2ft 3in-high Hutton Seam. Before I left school at the Glebe Seniors I hadn't really thought of what I would do, then on my way home from school one day I knocked on the door of the training officer and asked about a job. That was three weeks before I left school at Easter in 1967 and on the 10th April that year I started at the Glebe. I had to report to Dame Margaret's Hall in Washington for one week's surface training, so off I went with my towel rolled up under my arm with my pit clothes in. When I got there I couldn't see anyone knocking about, but I finally found someone to ask where I had to go.

'He ushered me through this door and there must have been at least 200 young lads starting at the pits just like myself. They'd come from all over Durham – and I thought that I'd be starting on my own! The next week I started on the screens picking the stones out of the coal. Normally this job was for youngsters like myself or for those who were on light work, having been injured and had come to bank. I can also remember working with men who were nearly retired and thinking they must have started work during the First World War.

'Some of them could hardly breathe, but I didn't realise it was coal dust that had done this to their lungs. I just accepted that if you were a miner you had a bad chest. How stupid can you get. Although I think on the whole our generation thought like that. We still had a bit of the First World War mentality.

'The first time I went down the pit was at Usworth Colliery in September 1967 when I was doing my 13 weeks underground training. Apprentices did six weeks at Usworth and seven weeks at Dame Margaret's Hall.

'What sticks in my mind is being shown how to work with the pit ponies. The one we had at Usworth was called Charlie, he was 28 years old and at that time he knew more about pit work than I did.

'We went on a visit to the Washington F Pit to the Victoria Seam which was only 18 inches high. Now that was an eye-opener. It was a coal hewing face down which all politicians should have been put for a shift. I wonder how they would have managed?'

Jim writes of his first shift: 'On 28th December 1967 at 2.15pm 'ah was abed' as Bobby Thompson would have said, but instead it was my first shift down the Glebe pit. Getting into the cage was an experience. It had two decks. The top one held 10-12 men and the bottom deck, which was only tub height, held 8-10 men. We had to sit on our hunkers. What a difference in later years when I worked at Wearmouth Colliery where the cage had three decks each of 50 men.

'A rush of air hit us as we passed the hole into the darkness. It was a smooth ride, just the sound of the cage knocking against the wooden skeeting as it guided it down the shaft, accelerating away, passing the other cage with men in on their way to bank. Sometimes we could hear them talking, lucky so and so's. As we neared the shaft bottom the cage would slow down and we'd land inch perfect. Binns' lift couldn't have done it better.

'I was surprised how clean and well lit it was. My first job was when the supposedly empty tubs came out of the cage. If they had any timber, girders etc. in, I would send them into the dish to dreg them up. The set lads would make them into sets and take them inbye. The rest I'd send up the creeper to the loader to be filled with coal, where they would be sent back to the cage to go to bank.

'It was freezing cold, especially in the winter, all that cold air coming down the shaft to go inbye to ventilate the workings. At bait time I'd go into the hauler house and get behind the water tank, which was red hot, to get warm.

'Sometimes when we were waiting on for coal I'd explore the old workings round the shaft. I'd go through the doors to the upcast shaft and along the "Burma Road" where the air was warm, dusty and foisty having travelled round the pit. I can smell it now.

'One day I was at the loader and was told: "Don't fill this tub". I was curious so I looked in the tub. Inside was a pit pony that had been killed inbye. It had been put in the tub to bring it out. What a pitiful sight it was, all bent up to get it into the tub. I remember that as much as anything else. What a waste. It didn't deserve an end like that. It should have been galloping round the fields enjoying life.

Jim Wilson with his wife Sonia during her visit to Wearmouth Colliery, Sunderland.

'The stables were at the shaft bottom and the ponies were treated really well. In the first stall was Clip, whose party piece was to suck a Black Bullet. He would slurp away at it. Another one was called Alfie. We'd ask him to count and he would paw the ground.

'After spending about a year at the shaft bottom I went inbye to work. Thank God to get away from that freezing area. The jobs varied from cleaning up spillage to manning a transfer point, which was where the coal was loaded from one belt to another. Now that was a boring job. The job I liked best was timber leading – taking the timber up the gates to the face. Some gates had a rope haulage system installed, but in others we used a pony and tram. We'd load the tram up and the pony would pull it in. Sometimes we'd fly in, but more often than not the pony would do it at his own pace, I think to show who was really the master! The ponies always knew when it was time to go outbye, then they would shift.

'It was one of the times we were going outbye that I'll always remember. The pony we had was called Hawk and we used to ride them out bare back. We'd get wronged if we were caught. As I was travelling out one of the lads asked me to take his pony as well because it was too small to ride. So off I galloped holding on to his pony by a rope, but halfway out the rope slipped from my fingers. I stopped, got off my pony and went back for the little one. I was just about to get back on Hawk when he galloped off. I was in a panic. He could go anywhere and get hurt, he was completely in the dark, he couldn't see where he was going and could have run into anything.

'I flew outbye looking for him, dragging the poor little pony behind me. I was in such a state. When I went to the stables to tell the horse-keeper what had happened, there was Hawk, standing in his stall none the worse for his adventure. I was lathered but at that moment over the moon to see him. He just looked as if to say: "What kept you?"'

Jim trained at Westoe for his face work and then started on the faces at the Glebe. He writes: 'I was 18 and Number 4 in the Hutton Seam. It was 2ft 3ins high, dowty props and heads. What a difference from Westoe, where the faces were fully mechanised with powered roof supports, a roof of steel.

We were as far back as the hills at the Glebe. Being warm we wore only shorts, vest, boots and stockings, and at the end of the shift we were black from head to foot.'

Jim tells of the 'thin veil of dust everywhere' at the face. He had no choice but to breathe it in. 'The worst place to work was the tailgate or caunch. With the direction of the ventilation we weren't just exposed to the dust we were making, but to everyone else's. The coal cutting machines were the worst offenders. The dust just billowed from them. When we were working in low seams it could not be dispersed easily. We were literally eating dust.'

Like all pitmen, Jim is well aware of the many disasters which have hit the coalfield. They included the Glebe Colliery tragedy of February 1908 when an explosion killed 14 men. He comments: 'When coal is cut methane is given off. This can accumulate where the ventilation is poor, such as in old workings or especially in the waste, which is the area that has been worked, behind the advancing face. When the barometer is high it is kept back by the air pressure and doesn't enter the normal ventilation where men are working, but when the barometer is low it has the opposite effect. The dangers are obvious. If there are sufficient quantities of approximately 5% to 15% of methane, then explosions can occur. Apart from that, there is the danger of oxygen levels falling with dire consequences.

'The Glebe disaster was a coal dust and firedamp explosion caused by shot firing. The shot hole had been overcharged. The initial firedamp explosion caused a coal dust explosion that is much more violent. It can travel at 1,000mph. The preceding wind goes head of the explosion, kicking the dust up and feeding it till its source of fuel is exhausted.

'After this, the great danger is carbon monoxide. That's

why canaries are taken underground. They are about six times more susceptible to carbon monoxide than a human being is, so if the canary falls off the perch it is time to withdraw to fresher air.'

Jim stresses the importance of ventilation. 'The efficient circulation of air is vital. Safety rules have arisen out of the many tragedies. The regulation book is written in blood.'

When the shift was over the miners were glad to get to the baths: 'It was lovely to stand under the shower after a hard shift, until you were washing your hair that is, because some joker would turn the water on to cold when you had soap in your eyes and you'd got the temperature right as well (I have to admit, though, that I was as guilty as anybody else!).

'And then you'd feel somebody washing your back, which you would do in turn for them. Even in the 1930s some, if not all, miners in Washington wouldn't wash their backs because they thought it weakened it. Instead, they would rub their backs with a piece of sacking.'

Of the Durham Miners' Gala, Jim writes: 'It was a day out for all the family, even if the menfolk went missing for a while. My first recollection is coming back from Durham with Washington F's banner, getting off the train at Usworth station and dancing behind the band all the way up to the New Inn corner and along Spout Lane to the Welfare. I must have been about five or six at the time.

'The first time I went with the Glebe was in 1967. I'd got my Durham money off the union in my pocket. I think it was only £2.10s but that was more than enough. Being only 15, I spent it all on the shows.

'I was lucky enough to carry the Glebe banner out of Durham in the Centenary Gala. By this time most of the pits in Durham had closed along with the Glebe. There was only a handful left. What a sight it was to see the old banners with the cobwebs dusted off and the mass of people having one last dance along the street. The beauty of it, the banners being free once more.

'I always think marching with the banner is akin to a guardsman trooping the colour. No guardsman could feel more pride.'

Jim Wilson collection

Miner Jim Wilson, of Usworth, Washington, with the Boldon Colliery NUM banner on Big Meeting day. Jim worked at the Glebe, Usworth, Boldon and Wearmouth collieries and did his face training at Westoe.

The Broken Thread

'I held my hand up in front of my eyes and I couldn't see anything at all.'
Jimmy Wilson

Jim Wilson's son, Jimmy, was taken on a trip down the mechanised Wearmouth Colliery shortly before it closed in 1993. This was a large, very modern pit. By this time, Jim was a deputy with an HNC in mining. Jim and his friend, Ray Lish, acted as guides.

Pointing to the second highest tower at Wearmouth, Jim explained: 'That's the C Pit, a man-riding shaft. We'll be descending that to 1,570ft. It goes deeper than that to 1,850ft. That's where the new reserves are. It's a shame that they'll be lost. They've only been in production a year.'

When Jimmy asked: 'What happens to coal once it's brought to the surface?' Jim replied: 'It gets unloaded from the D Pit and goes into the washer where it's washed to remove stone. Then it's transferred to eight, 1,000-tonne bunkers next to the river. From there it goes to the rapid loader from where the trains take it to Tyne Dock, and then the boats go to London.'

Jimmy described Jim's work clothes: 'On his feet were black, steel-toe capped safety boots. He was wearing orange overalls, the same type that had adorned our washing line every week for as long as I could remember. He had thick, black rubber protection pads on both knees. Around the belt on his waist was a self-rescuer, a miner's lamp and a black battery about the size of a small packet of soap powder. On his head was a white safety helmet with a retractable Perspex visor and ear protectors. A cable led from the battery on his waist to a light attached to the front of the helmet.'

It was now time for Jimmy and the other members of the group to get changed into mining clothes: 'I entered the locker and was struck by the sheer size of it. The place seemed enormous, divided into two parts, one side for dirty clothes and one side for clean clothes. In between the two sets of lockers were showers.' Before going down, Jimmy and the other visitors were told that if gases were detected they must use the breathing apparatus (self-rescuer) provided for them.

When they reached the cage, Jim explained: 'This is the man-riding shaft of the C Pit. It goes to all levels in the mine. The cage holds 150 men, 50 per deck. It will take us one and a half minutes to get to the 1570ft level at a speed of 40 foot per second. Please get ready to be searched before you enter.'

'It's just like the lift in Fenwick's man!' shouted one of the miners who had joined the group as they assembled in front of the cage.

The man in charge of the cage told them: 'I'm the banksman. Has anyone got digital or battery-operated wrist watches, cigarettes, watches or lighters. If you have, you must deposit them with me. Also, any foil or silver paper such as crisp packets or Kit Kat wrappers. It's illegal to take these items underground as they pose an explosion risk.'

Jimmy writes: 'As I held my arms up to be searched in the same way as if I was entering a football ground, I was reassured by the strict implementation of safety procedures.

'The cage seemed to move slowly at first into the gloom, punctuated only by the light of cap lamps, but rapidly picked up speed. This is more like Alton Towers than Fenwick's, I thought. After a short time the cage slowed down and we were greeted by two friendly miners who welcomed us into their underground domain. I was surprised how light and airy the place was. I looked around and saw that the walls and roof were painted bright white and the floor was a carpet of white dust. I kicked the dust up with my boots and my father interjected: "That's stone dust. Absorbs explosions and stops fires spreading. It won't be bright and clean when we're on the face.'"

A train driven by an electric engine took them towards the face. After a while, they were told they had just passed the three-mile mark and were under the sea. In fact, at this point they were under international waters.

Jimmy continues: 'I saw passageways snaking away from the main tunnel at regular intervals and occasionally we passed small groups of men who shouted to their friends as we passed. After half an hour of travelling the train stopped and we alighted. We assembled as a group again, joined by approximately 10 miners who were heading in the same direction as us.

'The air seemed more humid at this point and I began to sweat. Adjacent to the tunnel wall I could see a large conveyor belt approximately three feet wide constantly running with large blocks of coal on it. The coal on the belt seemed like blood coursing through a vein destined to feed the voracious appetite of the Thames power stations.

'Ray stated above the noise: "There are 19 miles of belts

Jim Wilson collection

Miner's son Jimmy Wilson in his younger days, standing beside the Washington F Pit Lodge banner on the Gala field.

that take the coal from the faces to the shaft. These have replaced ponies and tubs in most mines and they're linked to computers on the surface. The coal can also be stored in 1,500-tonne bunkers underground."

'Another miner added: "Aye, if the belts are standing we're knackered, the whole pit stops."

'We followed the belts for a mile until we reached a hole in the tunnel wall on the left. My dad gathered us together and spoke: "This is a gate, the entrance to a face. Remember, there's men working, so keep back when the shearer comes past. There's not much room, so keep down." Before entering the hole into unknown territory we put gloves on and crawled on our hands and knees. My father and I went in last.

'The tunnel was very narrow and the roof was only four feet high so standing up was impossible. The same roof supports that I had seen earlier on the surface were holding the roof up and stretched away into the dark distance. The only lights came from our cap lamps and there were puddles of water everywhere. To the right of us I saw a raised metal track and a gap of five feet and there it was, a massive wall of coal. The light of my lamp was glinting off the shiny edges. I could hear voices on an intercom shouting that they were ready to start work.

'My father said to the group: "Go on ahead I'll catch you up" and we were suddenly alone. He said: "This is an historic moment for me. My Dad did this with me when I was 15, and his dad before him. Switch your light off." I obeyed him and we were plunged into darkness. It was a darkness that I had never experienced before. I held my hand up in front of my eyes and I couldn't see anything at all. It was a very poignant moment and I felt as if a thread of continuity had been broken in my family for ever as I would never experience this again, certainly not with my offspring.

'We switched our lights back on as we heard a rumbling noise in the distance. I could make out lights and figures coming towards us as the noise got louder and louder. Soon the noise was deafening, like a constant crashing of rocks together and I saw the shearer for the first time.

'It was a magnificent sight, I thought. The shearer was a huge cylinder with spikes all around, spinning fast and advancing towards me. I pinned myself against the wall to allow the operator to crawl past me. I watched the shearer cut through the coal like a knife through butter, the coal falling effortlessly on to a belt behind. I saw jets of water spraying out from the machine, and I started to experience slight breathing difficulties.

'The air was thick with black dust and I could feel particles of grit in my eyes and mouth. The heat was incredible and I was sweating profusely. I observed that the miners following the shearer were bare-chested or only wearing vests. I was glad that I was wearing knee pads as sharp rocks protruded from the floor. Now I knew how my father's legs had blue scars on them, like veins in a Stilton cheese. This was caused by the coal dust getting into cuts.

'The shearer passed and rumbled off into the distance. I thought that we must have crawled at least half a mile and my throat and mouth were very dry. My father said: "Here, I've kept this," and he gave me a small bottle of coke. It was the best bottle of coke that I had ever had, as my mouth felt like sandpaper.

'The group gathered back together again. My father shouted: "Before the shearer comes back we have to move the roof supports forward and let the rock fall in. If we don't, the pressure on the face by the millions of tons of rock and water above us will squash us like ants. Could everyone put their ear muffs on?"

'I was fascinated by what was about to happen. As the miners moved each support forward into the gap created by the shearer I saw rocks come crashing down behind me. I could feel the floor, roof and walls shaking violently and the noise was unbelievable.

'One of the group asked my father how far the coal went. He replied: "We're seven miles off the coast now. The pit goes as far as nine miles out, but the coal goes as far as Norway."'

On the train back to the shaft, a miner told Jimmy: 'They're going to have to get their coal from Australia, Columbia and Poland now. Buy British! It's a bloody joke, man. This pit can produce a million tonnes of coal a year at a massive profit and they're putting us all on the dole. It doesn't make sense.'

Jimmy writes: 'From the tone of his voice, and all the other miners I spoke to that day, I could sense deep resentment and anger over the impending closure.'

Today, Jimmy plays cornet in the Craghead Colliery Band, which marches with the lodge banner at the Durham Gala. At the 2007 Big Meeting, the band was preceded by a former miner wearing the old pit clothes belonging to Jimmy's father.

Jim Wilson

Jimmy Wilson in the lamp room after his trip down Wearmouth Colliery shortly before the mine's closure.

The Last Face

'The whole decision to close Ellington is based on supposition and imponderables.'
Ian Lavery, NUM leader

Ellington Colliery was linked underground to its adjacent sister mine, Lynemouth. The first side of this combine to close was Lynemouth. Much of Ellington's coal went to the Alcan aluminium smelter, situated on the coast only a short distance from the pithead. Ellington closed in 1994 and the ponies were brought up for retirement, but the mine re-opened after only a few months, the Alcan smelter again being a key customer.

With the numerous pit closure of the 1980s and early 1990s, Ellington became the last deep mine in the North East. Between July 1991 and December 1993, Dawdon, Murton, Easington, Westoe, Vane Tempest and Wearmouth all ceased production.

Ellington now stood alone, the final remnant of a once great industry which had been central to the region's economy. By this time, the mine was owned by a private company – Britain's collieries had been privatised by the Conservatives.

The pit had always suffered from a water problem, but the difficulties were tackled and the undersea colliery became extremely productive. In 1983, its miners achieved a record output of one million tonnes in 29 weeks. Ellington also gained a record for the longest length of coal mined in a single shift.

On January 12, 2005, water began to flood the colliery's last working face, stopping all production. It was believed to be gushing from old, abandoned workings. Owners UK Coal said the problem was costing up to £80,000 a day in lost production. It was reported that water was filling the face and roadways at the rate of 1,350 gallons a minute.

Despite this, progress was made by the men in tackling the flood. The miners needed time. However, on January 26, 2005, Gerry Spindler, chief executive of UK Coal, met union officials, including NUM national president and chairman Ian Lavery, at the pithead.

The Journal newspaper, the regional daily based in Newcastle, reported that Mr Lavery and his colleagues were stunned when Mr Spindler opened the meeting with the words: 'Gentlemen, the pit is closed.' The article pointed out that 800 years of history had been ended with words which took barely three seconds to speak.

The Journal told its readers: 'Last night exhausted mineworkers – who have battled round the clock for two weeks in a desperate effort to tackle a flooding crisis – claimed they had been "kicked in the teeth" by the decision. Miners, union leaders and local MPs accused UK Coal of acting with "indecent haste" by pulling the plug on the 340-job pit despite real progress being made to bale out the floodwater. They accused Britain's biggest coal company of using the flooding as an excuse to close Ellington.'

The report added: 'Miners had been hoping yesterday's meeting would result in them being given more time to prove that the last deep mine in the region could be saved. But UK Coal says it has been forced into closing Ellington on safety

ncjMedia / The Journal

Sad day. Ellington miners march from the colliery with their branch banner following closure of the pit in 2005.

grounds and because of the "unacceptable risks" associated with extracting reserves close to the flooded production face.'

The Journal quoted Mr Lavery, a former Ellington miner, as saying: 'The whole decision to close Ellington is based on supposition and imponderables. We are beating the flooding problem and all we were asking for was another 10 to 20 days to clear the water and then make a decision based on fact and not just guesswork. Instead they have consigned 340 men to the dole.' The newspaper commented in a leader article that it was hard to see why the miners could not have been given 'just a little more time' to try to save the colliery.

A tribunal ruled that UK Coal failed to carry out the 90-day consultation period before closing Ellington. In March 2008 agreement was reached on compensation payouts for the miners.

ncjMedia / The Journal

Last of the North East deep mines. An Ellington Colliery headgear tower is demolished following closure.

Miner Richard Bradley, of Cramlington, has worked in the pits for 30 years, his service including Bates, Ashington and Ellington. He was one of the Ellington men to lose their jobs when the pit closed, and was among those who marched from the colliery behind the NUM lodge banner after the shutdown. Both his grandfathers were miners.

Richard remembers: 'The water was flooding on to the face from old workings above. It was probably from the Yard and Main seams of the Lynemouth pit. It came in hard at first, but by the time the closure was announced we had the water under control with pumps. There was no great danger. In my view, Ellington men were the best in the coalfield at controlling water. We had plenty of experience at it.

'The management had a good workforce. Everything they asked us to do, we did, including weekend working. The closure was totally unnecessary.'

Today, Richard works for three days a week at a pit in Nottinghamshire. He is one of the last Great Northern miners still toiling underground, just as his hard-working ancestors did. He is also one of a huge number of people throughout Northumberland and Durham whose forefathers worked in the pits.

Those ancestors, many of whom suffered so much, deserve to be remembered and held high in our esteem. The miners made the North East. They contributed a priceless sum to its social as well as economic development. From those cheerful men labouring in the dark seams sprang much of the region's warm, friendly spirit, which still endures in the hearts of its people. The miners are a part of us, our true marras. We owe them a debt we can never repay.

North East Mining – A timeline of major events (major disasters in red)

1239 Henry III grants Newcastle townsmen permission to dig for coal.

1605-1608 First recorded wooden waggonways for coal in North East, connected to the River Blyth.

1708 Fatfield Colliery disaster, 69 killed, explosion.

1725-6 Causey Arch, near Stanley, County Durham, built. World's oldest surviving railway bridge.

1790s Iron rails first recorded on a North East waggonway.

1800 Phineas Crowther, of Heaton, Newcastle, invents vertical single-cylinder steam winding engine. It is adopted at many North East collieries.

1812 Felling Colliery disaster, 92 killed, explosion.

1814 George Stephenson constructs his first steam locomotive at Killingworth Colliery workshops.

1815 Heaton Main Colliery disaster, 75 killed, inrush of water.

1815 Geordie and Davy safety lamps invented.

1831 Northumberland and Durham miners' strike under leadership of Thomas Hepburn. Employers agree to cut working hours for boys and abolish 'tommy' shops requirement.

1832 Second strike by Northumberland and Durham miners led by Hepburn. Mass evictions.

1835 Wallsend Colliery disaster, 102 killed, explosion.

1844 Third great strike by Northumberland and Durham miners. Mass evictions.

1844 Haswell Colliery disaster, 95 killed, explosion.

1860 Burradon Colliery disaster, 76 killed, explosion.

1862 New Hartley Colliery disaster, 204 killed, shaft blocked by engine beam fall. Worst North East disaster.

1864 Northumberland Miners' Association founded.

1866 First Northumberland Miners' Picnic held.

1869 Cancellation of the yearly Bond at Monkwearmouth Colliery following strike and court case.

1869 Durham Miners' Association founded.

1871 First Durham Miners' Gala held.

1872 Final abolition of yearly Bond.

1880 Seaham Colliery disaster, 164 killed, explosion.

1882 Trimdon Grange Colliery disaster, 74 killed, explosion.

1909 West Stanley Colliery disaster, 168 killed, explosion.

1912 National miners' strike for minimum wage. Stoppage lasts over five weeks.

1926 Great Lockout and General Strike.

1947 Coal mines nationalised.

1951 Easington Colliery disaster, 83 killed, explosion.

1984-85 The Great Strike, against pit closures.

1993 Wearmouth Colliery closes, last deep mine in Durham coalfield.

2005 Ellington Colliery closes, last deep mine in Northumberland coalfield and North East.

A selection of sources consulted

The Great Northern Coalfield 1700-1900, Frank Atkinson, Durham County Local History Society, 1966

A Radical Lawyer in Victorian England. W.P. Roberts and the Struggle for Workers' Rights, Raymond Challinor, I.B. Tauris & Co, 1990

The Pitmen of the Northern Coalfield, Robert Colls, Manchester University Press, 1987

Northumberland Miners' History 1919-1939, J. Davison, NUM, 1973

Banners of the Durham Coalfield, Norman Emery, Sutton, 1998

The Coalminers of Durham, Norman Emery, Sutton, 1998

The Death Pit (West Stanley, 1909), Eric Forster, F. Graham, 1969

The Pit Children, Eric Forster, F. Graham, 1978

The Miners of Northumberland and Durham, A History of Their Social and Political Progress, Richard Fynes, 1873

The Durham Miners 1919-1960, W.R.Garside, Allen & Unwin. 1971

The Art of Mining. Thomas Hair's Watercolours of the Great Northern Coalfield, Douglas Glendinning, Tyne Bridge Publishing, 2000

Steam and Speed: Railways of Tyne and Wear from the Earliest Days, Andy Guy, Tyne Bridge Publishing, 2003

Let No Wheels Turn. The Wrecking of the Flying Scotsman, 1926, Margaret Hutcherson, TUPS Books, 2006

Troubled Seams, J.E. McCutcheon, County Durham Books,1955

From Mine to Ministry: The Life Story of the Rt Hon Thomas Burt MP, T.C. Meech, 1910

A Personal Narrative of the Appalling Catastrophe at Hartley, T. Wemyss Reid, 1862

History of the Parish of Wallsend, William Richardson, 1923

Above and Below the Limestone – The Pits and People of Easington District, David Temple, TUPS Books, 2001

The Collieries of Durham, David Temple, TUPS Books, 1994

Thunder Underground. Northumberland Mine Disasters 1815-1865, Roy Thompson, Landmark Publishing, 2004

Collieries of Northumberland, J.T. Tuck, Index Books, 1993

A Great Labour Leader: The Life of the Rt Hon Thomas Burt, A.Watson, 1908

The Story of the Durham Miners, Sidney Webb, 1921

A History of the Durham Miners' Association 1870-1904, John Wilson, 1907

Coal Mining in County Durham, Durham County EEC Study Group, 1993

Newspapers
Newcastle Courant
Newcastle Weekly Chronicle
The Journal, Newcastle.
Evening Chronicle, Newcastle.
Northern Echo.
Sunderland Echo
Sunderland and Durham County Herald

Useful websites for mining history researchers
Durham Mining Museum (www.dmm.org.uk)
National Union of Mineworkers (www.num.org.uk)
Durham Aged Mineworkers' Homes Association (www.durhamhomes.org.uk)
North of England Institute of Mining and Mechanical Engineers (www.mininginstitute.org.uk)
Woodhorn Museum (www.experiencewoodhorn.com)
Beamish Museum (www.beamish.org.uk)

Authors' acknowledgements

The authors would like to thank the following miners and other mineworkers for their kind help and generosity in sharing their memories, experiences and knowledge with us and whose contribution to the book has been vital: Jim 'Harry' Lucas, Jim Wilson, Alec Anderson, John Douds, Roger Harrison, Keith Jones, the late Eddie Job, Ray Grew, Norman Lindsay, Terry Meadows, Billy Middleton, George Brown, Malcolm Barras, Frank Keerie, Robert Bourne, Brian Welsh, Winston Pile, Richard Bradley, Patrick Gilbert, Ron Harper, and Colin Finlay.

We would also like to extend our grateful thanks to the following miners' wives, daughters, sons and other relations who have been equally helpful: Dorothy Pattinson, Carol Douds, Sonia Wilson, Tina Job, Dorothy Barras, Betty McLaren, Madge Davies, Margaret Cockburn, Jean Brown, Mary Lyons, Jean Harrison, Doreen Gilbert, Jimmy Wilson, Jack Fletcher, Alan Green, Christopher Wood, John Parker, Mel Flanighan Junior, Phil Smith, Billy Briggs, Bob Dunn, and Ray Tilly.

The authors also extend their thanks to the following people and organisations for their kind help in the preparation of this book: Project photographers Tom Yellowley and Richard Smith; Dr Stafford M. Linsley, industrial archaeologist; artist George Robson, organiser, Durham Miners' Gala, and retired financial secretary Durham Area NUM; Ian Lavery, president and national chairman of the NUM; Dave Guy, president of the NUM North East Area and Durham Miners' Association; Dave Hopper, general secretary of the NUM North East Area and Durham Miners' Association; Deborah Welch, of Northumberland Area NUM; Thompsons Solicitors; Edna Wallace (nee Wearmouth); Brian Aitken, editor of *The Journal*, Newcastle; Paul Robertson, editor of the *Evening Chronicle*, Newcastle; the Rt Rev Dr David E. Jenkins, former Bishop of Durham; John Humble, former director of Durham Aged Mineworkers' Homes Association; Helen Sinden, of Durham Aged Mineworkers' Homes Association; Tony Henderson, North East historian, author and journalist; Jim Cuthbert, of Jarrow; Norman Emery, archaeologist, mining historian and author; Durham Aged Mineworkers' Homes Association; Northumberland Aged Mineworkers' Homes Association; The North of England Institute of Mining and Mechanical Engineers; Andy Guy, railway historian and author; Ray Marshall, *Evening Chronicle*; Michelle Pyle, of Newcastle Dog and Cat Shelter; Jim Perry, administrator of Durham Mechanics' Trust; Ron French; Peter Watson; Mark Blacklock; Paul Given; Alan Geggie; Sue Coulthard, of Northumberland County Council; the staff of Newcastle Libraries; Vanessa Histon of Tyne Bridge Publishing and last but by no means least Anna Flowers, Manager Tyne Bridge Publishing.

Select index